David Lundberg's new book *Our Ma* .... His choice of sources is impeccable. The reader can have absolute confidence that the descriptions he gives of the various aspects of our future life are totally consistent with the great body of research compiled over the last 150 years. This book would suit a wider variety of readers from the newly bereaved to those confronting their own mortality. Overall a magnificent achievement.

— Victor and Wendy Zammit, authors of
A Lawyer Presents the Evidence for the Afterlife

Award-winning author Lundberg follows up *Unifying Truths of the World's Religions* with a well-researched and thoroughly referenced text. Lundberg tackles complex concepts and comprehensively unpacks them to facilitate audience understanding. He pulls from a myriad of resources to help audiences embrace their fear of the unknown. This book, by its very nature and depth, will spark thought-provoking conversations that make it a surefire must-read.

— The US Review of Books

Our Magnificent Afterlife is a book whose time has come. It will open the door for many who are elderly and are very concerned for what is ahead. As a counselor for many who have faced their transition to the next life, I would have been very grateful to have such a book to give. This information is paramount for preparation for the end of life. It is well-written and easy to read. Congratulations for a great book of depth and breadth that will do much for people of all ages.

— Rev. Carl Showalter, Spiritual Director,
Spiritual Awareness Fellowship

Our Magnificent Afterlife is indispensable for anyone who wants to know what to expect when they leave this world for the next. All this wisdom comes from those who have actually experienced Heaven and gives us a step by step approach to this amazing and perfect experience that awaits all of us. I can assure you, after reading this book you will no longer have that greatest fear of all, the fear of death.

— Warren King, L.Ac, author of *The Soul's Journey:
A Pre-Life Adventure,* and *Love Your Organs, Love Yourself*

David Lundberg's excellent research brings to us, in a single volume, many detailed communications coming from those who are experiencing their magnificent afterlife, and those who have returned following near-death experiences to share their knowledge. David has beautifully organized these testimonials and teachings to answer our questions and to inspire us to seek even more. We don't have to wait. We can begin building *Our Magnificent Afterlife* here and now and make the most of our lives! I highly recommend it!

— Alberta V. Fredricksen, author of
Resume of a Disciple: Stepping Up Spiritually

A big and comprehensive work…a major undertaking reflecting a great deal of research.

— Professor Stafford Betty, author of *The Afterlife Unveiled*

Our Magnificent Afterlife: Beyond Our Fondest Dreams compiles information and excerpts from dozens of afterlife sources. It examines the promise of the Heaven World, how souls spend their time, the incredible beauty, mindpower, soul bodies, judgment, Purgatory, halls of learning, government, and numerous other afterlife aspects in its 55 chapters.

Lundberg's mission statement is in his introduction, *"My mission became to discover and share the best and most reliable descriptions about the afterlife and the best explanations for how it all works."* It synthesizes, under one cover, a treasure trove of knowledge about the many beautiful, loving, logical features found in the Heaven World.

No reader who believes in the afterlife should be without this thorough overview that describes the afterlife's organization, promises, and overall significance. This work offers hope, comfort and essential afterlife information for all who have concerns about what follows their lives on Earth.

— Midwest Book Review

Our Magnificent Afterlife

Beyond Our Fondest Dreams

Our
Magnificent
Afterlife

Beyond Our Fondest Dreams

C. David Lundberg

HeavenLight Press
Bozeman, Montana

Our Magnificent Afterlife
Beyond Our Fondest Dreams

C. David Lundberg

Print ISBN: 978-0-9796308-1-1
eBook ISBN: 978-0-9796308-3-5
Library of Congress Control Number: 2018914693

Printed in the United States of America

Front Cover Art: Tom Miller
Typesetting & Cover Design: Denis Ouellette

HEAVENLIGHT PRESS
P.O. Box 4071
Bozeman, Montana 59715

HeavenLightPress.com

DEDICATION

To those who hope for a better world.
To those who miss loved ones who have gone on.
And to those who may fear what lies ahead.
To all we say,

Be of good cheer,
for our Creator is a merciful and a loving God.
The Light conquers all, and you will be delivered
from all pain and sorrow.

CONTENTS

CONTENTS

PART III: QUESTIONS AND MISCONCEPTIONS
ABOUT THE AFTERLIFE

CONTENTS

PART IV: KEYS FOR SPIRITUAL ATTUNEMENT

INTRODUCTION

What does it feel like to be "dead?"

What do souls do in the afterlife?

What is the afterlife environment like?

Does the afterlife seem more or less real than Earth life?

How can I get to Heaven after all the sins I've committed?

*How does learning more about the afterlife
change a person's life?*

*Is there really a place prepared for us where beauty,
love, joy, and peace exceed our fondest dreams?*

These and many other thought-provoking questions are answered in this book about the afterlife—the life we find ourselves living after we pass from this life. What is greatly needed is for people to learn about the realities of the afterlife—the beauty there, the love, the fulfillment, and the peace. Knowing more about these future realities gives us more to look forward to, and more to live for. There is so much that is beautiful, permanent, and *real* to live for!

We take for granted so much in life. Many just see the visible creation, and don't consider the MAGNIFICENT DESIGN behind the physical. Most people don't fully comprehend how very blessed we are because of this, or what it fully means to have our All-Powerful, Wise and Loving Creator manifesting ever-growing goodness throughout the Universe. Once people comprehend the enormity of our stupendous blessings and unlimited potential, and what Our Creator's Grand Design is, life will be seen and enjoyed with far more hope and anticipation for our unending future. Also, once people understand how divine justice works within this Grand Design, the purposeful acts that cause suffering to others will diminish and Earth will be more Heaven-like.

Our lives have a glorious purpose, and the future for every reasonably good person (no, we don't have to be perfect) is much brighter than most of us realize. For those who want to transform their lives into something closer to Heaven on Earth—there are rich rewards for investing time in learning about our eternal future.

Our Magnificent Afterlife offers a compilation of some of the best information available about the afterlife, saving your valuable time so you don't have to hunt for it. Included is a collection of descriptions about what it's really like after we leave our physical bodies and proceed to either the "Summerland" level, the higher realms above the Summerland, or possibly the lower "Purgatory" levels reserved for temporary purification.

The Summerland is a permanent place where nearly all souls temporarily abide at some point in their evolution. It is also known as "Paradise," or the "Third Sphere." It is located, depending on which information sources are referenced, in the upper levels of the astral plane or the lower levels of the etheric plane, and we will consider these different "planes" in more depth later in this book. The Summerland is earthlike in many respects, but far more beautiful. It is a kind and loving place, where countless souls enjoy a myriad of activities. Several sources are used throughout the book to describe the beauty of the Summerland, the souls that reside there, and the love they share. One newly arrived soul in the afterlife describes it this way:

INTRODUCTION

Nothing which can enter into the creative imagination of a man while in the earth life can equal the glories which await his wondering intellect when he puts off the earth body.[1]

Currently, NDEs (near-death experiences) frame the majority of perceptions about the afterlife, as most books on this topic today are about NDEs. In contrast, research for this book included many reports from the early twentieth century when souls who have resided in the afterlife for some time reported back to us—and not just glimpses, but details about the many dimensions and the amazing beauty found there. These reports have come to us through telepathy and automatic writing. This book contains reports from these older sources as well as more recent NDEs, and provides a good cross-section of the numerous afterlife sources. Also, some of the afterlife researchers that have been quoted have each examined hundreds of different afterlife reports, providing significant corroboration of what is presented. To learn about the sources used, refer to "The Purity and Accuracy of our Sources" in the Appendix.

I offer the following research with the greatest sincerity and a deep humility. All the quotations and my commentary herein are designed to provide clear and logical explanations about the afterlife, our Creator, and certain afterlife experiences that await us.

My search for information about God, the meaning and purpose of life, who we really are, and what happens after death began at a very young age, but not until my college years did anything significant happen. When I was twenty years old I was experiencing a time of deep discouragement because I had not found the answers I'd been seeking about God and the reason for being. I was lying in bed, feeling quite blue, and said a prayer for help—an emotional, pleading prayer. Then, it happened.

In the upper right-hand corner of my bedroom a very bright light appeared, growing bigger. It matched the numerous descriptions I have since found in many NDE accounts, of a light "brighter than the sun," yet it didn't hurt my eyes. I received no verbal messages, but I was filled with positive energy: a tremendous dose of pure light and love! I immediately felt quite well again which was accompanied with a new sensation of energy. Any doubts I had about the existence of God, or the existence of Heaven, left me forever. I feel very blessed for being able to have had that experience. This description may be quite difficult for some readers to believe. It is deeply personal to me, and I cannot provide any proof to others that it happened. I simply testify that it is a knowledge that has sustained me ever since.

Decades later, after studying many of the world religions, and being blessed with occasional spiritual revelations, I asked myself, "What does the world most need?" The answer, for me, was to write the book, *Unifying Truths of the World's Religions*, which highlights thirty-three principles confirmed by hundreds of quotations from the sacred texts of the world's major religions, and which contain important life lessons and spiritual truths. These principles are ones that can easily be embraced by people of all faiths.

While the sacred texts of the world religions all acknowledge the existence of an afterlife, or Heaven, they do not provide much detail about what it is really like once we get there. In pursuit of further insight, I studied numerous books about the afterlife for several years, both contemporary as well as those written a century or more ago. I was amazed to discover how much information is available on the subject, much of it quite credible and logical in its consistency and provided by a large number of different sources.

Despite all the information available, many people are unaware of how truly benevolent, merciful, loving and glorious God and eternal life are. Many of the best books about the afterlife, written in earlier times, have been forgotten. These older books need to be included for a thorough examination of what happens after we pass from this world. They contain descriptions from souls who reside in the afterlife, allowing them to supply much more detail than many NDEs are able to provide.

My mission became to discover and share the best and most reliable descriptions about the afterlife and the best explanations for how it all works. I was motivated by the many powerful benefits people will receive from this knowledge.

One primary benefit is how profoundly this information can lessen the pain of losing a loved one. Most of us have suffered such a loss, and this grief and sadness can be almost unbearable, even life-threatening. *Knowing* (not just hoping or believing) that life does not end at "death," and that God has prepared countless beautiful environments for our ongoing life, filled with meaningful things to do in loving service, as well as the enjoyment of loving relationships and pleasurable pastimes, is comforting for all who are now missing someone dear.

The incredible benefits of learning what happens next after this life are demonstrated by those who have returned from brief visits to the other side, having had a near-death experience. These people have, in most cases, significantly increased their loving service to others and their enjoyment of life on Earth. They have no more fear of death. They also have more courage to lead a more fulfilling life, engaging in public speaking or other activities that, before visiting the afterlife, would have felt too daunting. Most NDE'ers enjoy a greater sense of empathy and love in a broader circle of relationships.

The resulting freedom from the fear of death means that our remaining life in embodiment will be easier and more enjoyable. An increased motivation and enthusiasm to apply spiritual law amplifies loving relationships and the appreciation of the beauty in life. In addition, our souls are elevated, so upon transition to the next dimension of existence, we arrive at a higher, more beautiful level in the afterlife.

From the afterlife, Monsignor Robert Hugh Benson described the experience of a newly arrived soul into the Summerland area of the afterlife. (Information on Monsignor Benson can be found in chapter 2 and the Appendix.)

His first impressions upon his awakening in the spirit world were—to use his own words—absolutely breathtaking. He had visualized, subconsciously perhaps, some sort of misty state as the condition of a future life, where there would be a great deal of "prayer and praise." To find himself in a realm of inexpressible beauty, with all the glories of Earthly nature purged of its Earthliness, refined and eternalized, with the enormous wealth of colour all around and about him; to behold the crystal purity of the rivers and brooks, with the charm of the country dwellings and the grandeur of the city's temples and halls of learning...was to cast doubts upon the veracity of his own eyes.[2]

Visualize the most beautiful place you have seen on Earth, then multiply that beauty by a large number—significantly expand that loveliness. The beauty that exists in most areas of the afterlife far surpasses the most beautiful places on Earth! Many detailed descriptions of the Summerland are given in Part II, "Descriptions of the Afterlife."

Knowing what to expect makes our transition much easier. We will also enjoy freedom from the fear of judgment, by learning of the mercy and forgiveness regarding our inevitable mistakes in life.

There is another huge benefit from learning more about the afterlife—the *anticipation* of what awaits us. Just as a significant part of the fun of traveling is looking forward to it ahead of time—well, we are all going to go on a BIG trip! We all know that our physical bodies only last so long. But thank God that our eternal consciousness and our souls are *not* dependent on the physical world. We can experience the joy of knowing that life will be more meaningful and happier, and that all the beauty and goodness of life, including *feeling* so much better—will be *magnified* for all good people.

God loves his children and does not expect them to avoid mistakes. This has been confirmed by the great religious figures throughout history. Our Creator is loving, understanding, and merciful. He has provided unlimited pathways to more beautiful, loving, and peaceful environments in the afterlife commensurate with our progress. Our true, divine nature is goodness.

Some of my goals in presenting this afterlife information are:

- To help others increase their belief in and knowledge about God.

- To help more people believe in the afterlife, become more excited about it, and include it in their *vision of the future*. To establish that life offers so much to anticipate, that all good people can look forward to an awesomely magnificent future, filled with meaning, beauty, and love.

- To offer descriptions about what it is like there, and an understanding of how logical the design of the afterlife is.

- To give others something to believe in, to help them lose their cynicism, apathy, hopelessness, and their idolatry. (Sadly, so many people who are beset with difficulties cannot see and consequently, don't believe in a significantly better future.) The truth about the afterlife will help lighten the darkness in which so many are mired. This illumination will lift us up emotionally and spiritually.

- To establish the fact that divine justice reigns supreme, despite the apparent lack of it on Earth. Afterlife teachings reveal that there are divinely just consequences for causing suffering to any part of life. The afterlife teachings explain the truth about divine justice—how and why evildoers *will* regret their sins.

This keys into the anger and frustration so many are feeling today regarding the suffering caused by a relative few.

Let's face it. We are now living in a time when lies and corruption are being exposed on practically a daily basis. In addition, this is an era when Hollywood makes a few great movies each year, when the television networks make a few great shows each year, but the rest wastes our time and focuses our attention into the wrong places, such as senseless cruelty and violence and other demeaning and loveless forms of human interaction.

Many aspects of life on Earth at the present time are crude. At the level of our soul, we feel burdened by our culture that has little spiritual foundation. This is why spiritual seekers have a deep desire to know the true meaning of life and need to know what happens after we leave Earth.

Life offers so much to anticipate, to look forward to, if we would only invest more of our time and attention on what is good and true—namely, our spirituality.

The afterlife information in this volume provides an overview of the lower heavens that is more complete than most books on the subject. This book contains over one hundred and seventy excerpts from thirty-five different sources, with commentary. It provides easy-to-read and logical descriptions of the afterlife for all readers.

Some of the quotations in the book refer to a person or a soul as "he." When this convention is used, it is for ease of reading. Full and total inclusion of both genders are meant. The same applies when God is referred to as "He," or "Father," as God's attributes are simply not limited by gender. God's compassionate, nurturing, comforting, loving and creative nature certainly embody what we associate with feminine characteristics.

Many direct quotations from souls living in the afterlife are included, as their most important points and expressions are best left in their own words. Statements from afterlife sources that simply did not seem logical or were just too confusing are not included.

It is understandable that with the lack of "empirical evidence" a degree of healthy skepticism is appropriate. We are dealing with the vastness of Creation, after all, and it is folly to imagine that human science can ever encompass all of existence. Fortunately, there is a remarkable compatibility and consensus within afterlife accounts of what to expect, and these sources are not only independent from one another but have been reported during different times.

Our Magnificent Afterlife is an overview, a framework that describes the way Divine Intelligence (God in Action) has established such a beautiful and awesome eternal life situation for all good people. The afterlife *exists,* and readers will benefit from descriptions and explanations about it. Can we not achieve the regeneration of all people through the true knowledge of our collective spiritual destiny? Things are not supposed to stay the way they are in the physical world. We need to mesh with the higher spiritual dimensions. Then, humanity as a whole will reach new heights of health and happiness.

Each one of us must desire, seek out and prove for ourselves the truths we choose to live by. To those who objectively focus on the abundant evidence with an open mind, the reality of the afterlife is beyond question. Victor Zammit, a retired attorney and long-time investigator of over twenty different categories of afterlife evidence, states it simply and powerfully:

There is undeniable scientific evidence today for the afterlife…. After these many years [23] of serious investigation, I have come to the irreversible conclusion that there is a great body of evidence that absolutely proves the case for the afterlife. In fact I am stating that the evidence taken as a whole constitutes overwhelming and irrefutable proof for the existence of the afterlife.[3]

The existence of an afterlife filled with love, beauty, and fulfillment in joyful occupations may sound *too good to be true*. Many people claim that "scientific proof" of Heaven or the afterlife doesn't exist. They discount the many different categories of evidence available, or don't even look for them. For various reasons they choose not to believe. Perhaps they simply choose not to seek and find.

There are open-minded scientists, who despite the danger to their reputation, affirm the reality of the afterlife. In contrast, there are scientists who deny its existence without open-minded investigation. Dr. Robert Crookall comments on these scientists and cites Dr. Alfred Wallace, in Crookall's comprehensive book, *The Supreme Adventure:*

Those who sweep all aside, without systematic investigation, unconsciously use the a priori argument. Dr. Alfred Russell Wallace, the co-discoverer, with Charles Darwin, of Evolution, observed: 'The whole history of science shows that whenever scientific men have denied the facts of other scientific investigators on a priori [presumed] grounds of absurdity or impossibility, the deniers have always been wrong.'[4]

History has shown that those who discover new truth have always started from having a perspective of being an "open-minded skeptic." If a person is open to the possibility of the existence of God, and that God loves His children, they will, through study and meditation be open to and discover the Divine Presence in their heart.

Do look for reasons, if you will, why the following reports from the afterlife might not be true. Consider thinking twice, however, before settling on either of these two ideas: "It's beyond God's capability," or "This sounds too good to be true!" Our Creator is All-Powerful and loves His Creation surely more than we can comprehend from our mundane human vantage point.

This is why the subtitle "Beyond Our Fondest Dreams" was chosen. No matter how glorious and beautiful we might imagine the higher levels of the afterlife to be, the remarkable reports and testimonials make plain that our minds simply cannot grasp the uplifting, soul-elevating feelings, sights, sounds, light, and love that our Creator has prepared for us.

So, let us *embrace* our spirituality and who we really are: sons and daughters of God. Let us *embrace* the joyful anticipation of eternal life, the comforting certainty that in the heaven-world what awaits us are unending positive learning experiences and joyous fulfillments beyond our present imagination.

Let us accept this higher and truer reality, this dawning realization of the blessed afterlife our benign and loving Creator has fashioned for us. Let us gradually immerse ourselves within our true spiritual nature, turning our fear and trepidation of what awaits us after we pass from our earthly forms into an abiding sense of security, peace and acceptance of the wonders of our onward journey. And, we can also help our loved ones awaken to these blessings just beyond this earthly sojourn. Thus, we can in our own humble way, help reduce the darkness and suffering on Earth.

Read on to discover how God loves His children so very much as shown by *His Magnificent Divine Design* of the heaven-worlds. And read on to experience the comfort and joyful anticipation of knowing how very much our futures will be enhanced by the bliss of divine loving light flowing through us as we share it with our brothers and sisters.

Greater joy, sharing love and fulfillment are readily available—all that's required is learning about it, *believing* in it, *living* it, and *giving* it to others. *Embrace the glorious reality of God's Love! Enjoy reading about Our Magnificent Afterlife!*

PART I

GATEWAY
TO THE AFTERLIFE

❦ 1 ❦

Religions Convey God's Promise

This afterlife research is not about religion; rather, it is about our eternal life in spirit. Nevertheless, it is fitting to point out that the world's great religious traditions each state there is existence after death. A well-known quote from the Christian Bible addresses this:

> In my Father's house are many mansions: if it were not so, I would have told you. I go to prepare a place for you.[5]

The original Greek word for "mansions" was translated as "a stopping place." Scholars have concluded that Jesus was referring to a wide range of stopping places in the afterlife, in fact, a multitude of realms, spheres, planes, or dimensions of existence. As we explore this we will realize that many afterlife sources describe souls moving on into various higher levels of greater love and beauty.

Judaism, Islam, Buddhism, Hinduism, Jainism, Theosophy and other religions and spiritual belief systems have also stated or at least hinted at the existence of various levels in the afterlife. When souls leave the Earth, they do so after achieving various degrees of spiritual attainment, of knowledge, and an ability to love and forgive. It is understandable that differing afterlife planes or dimensions exist to provide environments that will best support every soul at their own level.

The sacred texts of the world's religions were written in ancient times. Since then, we have been graced with much new information. Today, many students of religion as well as many academics believe we are entering a new age of enlightenment—and this despite all the chaos being caused by those who seek to preserve and grow their wealth and power. Just as we witness astounding breakthroughs in all of the material sciences, this is equally a time of the unveiling of greater truths about our spiritual nature. It is important to not be so distracted by the mundane necessities of daily life that we miss out on the progressive revelations of our divine identity being revealed.

We become what we focus on, so let us focus as much as possible on what is good and beautiful. Let us view this lifetime for what it really is, a preparation for a far more meaningful and wonderful start to a fulfilling eternal life.

2

Our Brethren in the Afterlife Want Us to Know the Truth

In her book *Embraced by the Light*, Betty Eadie said she learned the following when she visited the afterlife during her near-death experience.

> They told me that it is important for us to acquire knowledge of the spirit while we are in the flesh. The more knowledge we acquire here, the further and faster we will progress there. Because of lack of knowledge or belief, some spirits are virtual prisoners of this earth. Some who die as atheists, or those who have bonded to the world through greed, bodily appetites, or other earthly commitments find it difficult to move on, and they become earth-bound. They often lack the faith and power to reach for, or in some cases even to recognize, the energy and light that pulls us toward God.[6]

It is logical that God wants us to know that a glorious future awaits us after we leave this Earth. Without such knowledge, where is the meaning in life? To what end do we suffer, experience failure, struggle, and die? Without such knowledge, we are wide open to despair and heartache. Should we suffer in ignorance when there is so much evidence for meaning and purpose in life?

The following are all *direct quotes* from souls who live in the afterlife, who have conveyed their messages through human contacts on Earth. If this concept is new to the reader, consider that since ancient times innumerable testimonials of such communications have been compiled. And while some are of little or no credibility, and even admitted fabrications, there are many that have a basis in observable fact. These latter have been studied to such an extent that facts and circumstances asserted by the communicators from the spirit world have been subsequently verified and independently confirmed here on Earth.

Monsignor Robert Hugh Benson (1871–1914) was the son of the Archbishop of Canterbury. He is the source of several respected and popular works about the afterlife. His messages were received and recorded by his friend Anthony Borgia, a gifted and well-known medium. (For more information about Monsignor Benson and other sources, see the Appendix). In the following excerpt, he shares the importance of learning about the afterlife:

The percentage is low, deplorably low, of people who come into the spirit world with any knowledge at all of their new life and of the spirit world in general. All the countless souls without this knowledge have to be taken care of, and helped in their difficulties and perplexities.... It is a type of work that appeals to many of the ministers of the church of whatever denomination. Their experience upon Earth stands them in good stead, and all of them...know that we are now members of one ministry, with one purpose, serving one cause, and all of us possessed of the same knowledge of the truth of spirit life, without creed, without doctrine or dogma, a united body of workers, men and women.[7]

It is clear that those who do not know anything about their inevitable afterlife future would benefit greatly from such knowledge. The soul of sister Frances Mary Banks, using telepathic communication with her close friend Helen Greaves after Bank's death in 1965, tells us how fear must be vanquished, and that the "veil between the worlds" should be removed:

People living on Earth, the erudite, the cultured and clever minds, as well as the devotional and religious minds, and the uneducated, the illiterate and the closed minds, must all be reached. All need this knowledge to remove fear which is one of the darkest and most powerful Earth-emotions which has to be fought and conquered before peace and progress can come to the Earth.[8]

If we had a significant increase in the number of people who knew about the beauty and joy that awaits all good people, and who knew the reasonable requirements of right living that align with our true divine nature, our world would transcend much of the current chaos and reach a higher level of peace, beauty and love, with much less suffering. Monsignor Benson had this also to say:

It is not a pleasant sight to see these gentle, patient helpers [in the afterlife] wrestling mentally—and sometimes almost physically—with people who are wholly ignorant of the fact that they are "dead." It is a most saddening sight.... Most of these souls blame themselves when they have been here long enough to appreciate their new conditions, or alternatively, they blame the world they have but recently left [our Earth] for tolerating such blindness and stupidity.[9]

The power of love to heal all wounds and to energize one's life is touched upon in this next message from the soul of Julia Ames, as received by her friend the Honorable William T. Stead.

You do not know the volume of refreshing water that will rush forth if you...save this people from perishing in the arid wilderness of unbelief.... I am speaking about love. There is love in this world like the water in the sea. Its waves are wailing and sobbing on the shore of human life; but you cannot hear, you do not understand. Why not try to flood your world with this heavenly love?[10]

There are many different levels of vibrations or dimensions in the afterlife. This experience of love would not necessarily apply to all souls immediately after they leave the physical body behind. If a soul chose to spend his life on Earth committing acts that were not loving, and did not desire loving relationships, that soul, upon "death" would very possibly not experience a world filled with love upon his initial arrival. Sooner or later, however, the love and forgiveness of others would provide this soul the opportunity to move on toward experiencing this loving environment.

We next hear from the mother of the Reverend G. Vale Owen, the Vicar of Orford, Lancashire, England, who wrote down his mother's communications from the afterlife:

Now it is no small matter that men should so live their lives on Earth that when they step over the threshold into the larger, freer sphere they should take up and continue their service in the Kingdom without a more or less protracted hiatus in their progress. We have seen the effect of the career of so many, as it is viewed in extension into this land, that we feel we cannot too much emphasize the importance of preparation and self-training while opportunity offers. For so many do put off the serious consideration of this, with the idea of starting afresh here, and when they come over they find that they had very little realized what that starting afresh really implied.[11]

The point here is the importance of realizing the truth of the afterlife *now*, to prepare for it *now*. There are some aspects of creating a good character and attuning to the natural joy of helping others, *while on the Earth now,* which are more difficult to accomplish in the afterlife. Why? It is because there are far more difficult challenges here on Earth that provide significantly greater opportunities to develop mastery over such situations. For this reason, it can be argued that it is actually *more difficult* to forge a good character in the afterlife than it is on Earth. It is harder to develop, grow, evolve and improve oneself there than here, because here we have tangible problems and challenges to overcome, such as are not present in the afterlife.

Our planet would certainly be raised up if more people truly believed and kept in the forefront of their consciousness that life goes on after we leave our physical body and that what we do here now is extremely important to our future. From the afterlife, Julia Ames tells us:

You are, in the loom of time, weaving the fabric of this world [your eternal afterlife experience].... You do it day by day, you do it hour by hour. You make your next life....

For there is here [when you enter the afterlife] no sudden transformation. You are as you were. There is no break of continuity. You start where you left off. What you are you remain.[12]

There is a widespread belief among those who do believe in an afterlife that significant changes take place—and that is true regarding many aspects, including the difference in the environment. However, one extremely important thing that does *not* change instantly is our pattern of thinking and the habits that underlie this thinking. Our habits require time and effort to improve. Several examples of this will be given throughout this book.

The following statements from Monsignor Benson reiterate the need for greater communication between the Earth and afterlife worlds, pointing out the need for greater afterlife knowledge.

...Neither was it intended that the two worlds, ours and yours, should be as they are now, so far apart in thought and contact. The day will assuredly come when our two worlds will be closely interrelated, when communication between the two will be a commonplace of life, and then the great wealth of resources of the spirit world will be open to the Earth world, to draw upon for the benefit of the whole human race....

It is to the eternal shame of the Earth world that so many souls should arrive here in woeful ignorance of what lies before them.... It is astonishing how many of them want to rush back to the Earth-plane to try to tell those they have left behind of the dis-

covery they have made of the fact that they are alive and in another world![13]

The world of spirit is more beautiful than we can imagine. Souls who abide there try very hard to help us here on Earth by transmitting comfort, energy, and wisdom where it is most needed.

What God wants for His children is for us to use our free will to focus on and implement all that is truth, beauty and goodness. We can be powerfully inspired to do so when we learn more about the glorious goodness in our future afterlife environment. We truly have unlimited potential to become more joyous, powerful, and overflowing with love. This process requires some time and effort but is exceedingly worthwhile.

❦ 3 ❦

How *Delightful* the Afterlife Is!

There is so much to look forward to in the afterlife, including the anticipation of growing spiritually by doing good works for others. It is a place of equal opportunity—opportunities on a scale grander than we can imagine for engaging our time. There is no need to earn a living, no need in fact to provide the body with food, drink, clothing, or housing. Souls are filled with happiness and gratitude. Although there is no need to work to survive, souls have a natural desire to occupy themselves in various ways that are pleasurable. The primary way is to experience the joy of helping others. In addition to helping others, souls enjoy the astounding beauties of their environment, studying their favorite subjects, music and the arts, exploring, and recreation.

Imagine doing what you do for the *sheer joy* of serving others, and not having to worry about money or health problems! God, our Loving Father, is the Creator of great goodness. We can and will be eternally grateful for the wonderful afterlife He has created for His children.

Sister Frances Banks describes the levels of the Summerland and higher levels this way:

Beauty is manifest, where negative or unkind thoughts are prohibitive because such thoughts are visible and audible, where help and love are always at hand to help the traveler, and where every circumstance points to a greater Life, a wider understanding and the glorious certainty of progress after effort and exertion.

This is an existence in another dimension of thought; disease, poverty, cruelty, suffering as it is known on Earth could not possibly exist here, because the Light of the Spirit opens our vision and we seek the Way to Higher Worlds of even more glorious beauty.[14]

William Stead, through his hand, previously provided us with a message from Julia Ames. After he himself entered the afterlife he had the following to say through Pardoe Woodman based on his direct experience:

It is only the spiritual and mental knowledge and development which hinders and advances the individual here....

It is a land of freedom. A land of happiness and smiles. A land of happiness brought about through the real love of man for man. A land to work for—a land in which your place is made according to the knowledge you have had whilst upon Earth and the way you have used that knowledge.

It is impossible to over-emphasize the degree of freedom in this new world, and the joy each and all has in it.[15]

The preceding excerpt touches on the importance of our personal development while we are still living on Earth. What we can learn from our fellow souls in the afterlife, and how we apply that knowledge while still on Earth will greatly influence our environment and companionship after we make our transition.

Monsignor Benson describes for us the recreational environment in the afterlife:

The most noticeable difference between our two worlds, in this matter of recreations, is created by our respective requirements. We have no need here to take bodily exercise, vigorous or

24

otherwise, nor do we need to go out into the "fresh air." Our spirit bodies are always in perfect condition, we suffer no disorders of any kind, and the air, which cannot be other than fresh, penetrates into every corner of our homes and buildings, where it fully retains its purity. It would be impossible for it to become impaired or contaminated in any way. It is to be expected, then, that our recreations should be more upon the mental plane than upon the "physical...."

We find that we have so much to learn, and learning is in itself such pleasure that we do not need the number or variety of recreations that you do. We have plenty of music to listen to, there are such wonders in these lands that we want to know all about, there is so much congenial work to be done, that there is no cause to be cast down at the prospect of there being few of the earthly sports and pastimes in the spirit world. There is such a superabundant supply of vastly more entertaining things to be seen and done here, besides which a great deal of the earthly recreations appear sheer trivialities.[16]

Once souls reach a certain level in the "Higher Realms" beyond the Summerland, a level of peace and joy is attainable that is beyond description. Sister Frances Banks describes her state after entering higher dimensions.

It is the Reality of Being. It is joy beyond words. It is in truth an ecstasy of living, of being a live, alert Self in a world of Live and Glorious Selves within a consciousness of a Great Creative Self.[17]

Sir Arthur Conan Doyle, the famous author of the Sherlock Holmes detective stories and respected author of spiritualist works, had the following to say about the experience that results from knowledge of divine truth and the afterlife:

Do we not begin to understand that "House with many mansions," and realize Paul's "House not made with hands," even as we catch some fleeting glance of that glory which the mind of man has not conceived neither has his tongue spoken?

It [the afterlife] all ceases to be a far-off elusive vision and it becomes real, solid, assured, a bright light ahead as we sail the dark waters of Time, adding a deeper joy to our hours of gladness and wiping away the tear of sorrow by assuring us that if we are only true to God's law and our own higher instincts there are no words to express the happiness which awaits us.[18]

H. W. Engholm, the editor of Reverend Owen's book series, offers an overview of the afterlife:

We find trees and flowers like those that grow in earthly gardens, but more beautiful, immune from decay and death, and endowed with qualities that make them more completely a part of our lives. Around us are birds and animals, still the friends of man, but nearer, more intelligent, and freed from the fears and the cruelties they suffer here [on Earth].

We find houses and gardens, but of substance, color and atmosphere more responsive to our presence... wide-ranging harmonies of color. We find everything more radiant, more joyous, more exquisitely complex, and while our activities are multiplied, our life is more restful.

Differences in age disappear. There are no "old" in the Spheres of Light; there are only the graceful and strong.[19]

It was reported that the soul of Samuel Wilberforce, Bishop of Winchester, came through Father Stainton Moses, a Priest of the Church of England and a medium, answering the question "Are the spheres like this world [the Earth]?" The following answer was received:

In every way similar. It is only the change of conditions that makes the difference. Flowers, and fruits, and pleasant landscapes, and animals, and birds, are with us as with you. Only the material conditions are changed. We do not crave for food as you; nor do we kill to live. Matter, in your sense, is done with; and we have no need of sustenance, save that which we can draw in with the air we breathe. Nor are we impeded in our movements by matter, as you are. We move freely, and by volition. I learn by degrees, and as a newborn babe, to accustom myself to the new conditions of my being.[20]

In the Summerland, there are Halls of Learning for every subject that could be of interest and not opposed to spiritual law. In these halls, the laws of life are studied, as well as the nature of problems in life. Minds are trained and intuition is developed. All who wanted to pursue studies further while on Earth, but were unable to, now have the opportunity to do so. (See chapters 29–31, "Halls of Learning," "Colleges of Music and the Arts," and "Halls of Science.")

The Summerland is reported to have beautiful lakes, rivers and seas for our enjoyment. The waters are described as alive with their own intelligence. And with movement, they create soft beautiful music that blends harmoniously with all other sounds in the environment. The waters joyfully create music to praise God![21]

It is reported that the environment is perfectly suited for us in the afterlife and provides maximum comfort. Additionally, in the Summerland and levels beyond, souls enjoy a wonderful sense of well-being. The following description is from Monsignor Benson:

It is impossible to convey, even in a small measure, this exquisite feeling of supreme vitality and well-being. When we are living upon the Earth-plane we are constantly being reminded of our physical bodies in a variety of ways—by cold or heat, by discomfort, by fatigue, by minor illnesses, and by countless other means. Here we labor under no such disabilities. By that I do not mean that we are just unfeeling logs, insensible to all external influences, but that our perceptions are of the mind, and that the spirit body is impervious to anything that is destructive....

All is exactly attuned to its inhabitants—its temperature, its landscape, its many dwellings, the waters of the rivers and streams, and, most important of all, the inhabitants one with another. There is therefore nothing that can possibly create any unhappiness, unpleasantness, or discomfort. We can completely forget our bodies and allow our minds to have free play, and through our minds we can enjoy the thousands of delights that the same minds have helped to build up.[22]

Most importantly, in the afterlife world of the Summerland and beyond, one can feel much closer with God. All grateful hearts can more readily feel the presence of God within themselves and throughout their environment.

In the Summerland, as we have said, life is much easier due to the lack of any need for food and drink. It appears that sleep is only required by some souls upon first arriving, as part of the healing and transition process. There is no night, so the sense of time is changed due to not having night to break up day; there is just one ongoing "day."

There is no illness of the finer body that the soul inhabits. (See chapter 16, "The Spiritual Body.") There is hardly ever fatigue, unless extremely challenging tasks are undergone for long periods. There is plenty of opportunity for rest and relaxation, should it be needed.

Many of the delights of the Summerland are simply accepted with thanks. How they have been created is not fully understood by the inhabitants. Our loving Father provides all good things, all that souls require, to move on in spiritual evolution. Based on several reports from souls living in the afterlife and others who have visited there, words cannot fully describe these various awe-inspiring beautiful realms of Heaven!

SUICIDE IS NOT AN OPTION! Even though the afterlife is truly "heavenly," the saints and avatars warn us that we must not do anything, including suicide, which would shorten our time on Earth. Our current lifetime on Earth is a precious gift, a profound opportunity to resolve past failures and damaged relationships, a time to give back to life and thereby prepare ourselves for a wonderful future in the Hereafter.

Furthermore, the great traditions teach us that our body temples are sacred. It is our responsibility to take the very best possible care of these Temples of the Spirit. For example, if we know certain foods are not healthy to eat, it is best to avoid them. Instead of surrendering or giving up in the face of pains, infirmities, and limitations, we need to persevere on Earth. It is important for those in pain or who are troubled to seek out help from wise and loving counselors.

The Christian Saints and wisdom teachers have all spoken of the immense grace and blessings that come to us when we accept even the most severe trials and tribulations with courage, dignity, and patience. Suicide literally robs the souls of spiritual attainment.

Noted medium Mrs. M. T. Longley, a spiritual lecturer from the early twentieth century, issued a warning against any consideration of suicide to those who may be eager to start their afterlife adventure before they should.

[The change of death is] not one to be voluntarily sought, not one to be gained by suicide, for that step would defeat the desired end by enmeshing the spirit in the web of Earthly conditions, but one to be graciously accepted when Nature works her will with the worn-out body.[23]

Suicide in most cases will cause great sorrow and regret in the soul that does so, as well as cause pain and grief for their loved ones. (There is no law against the use of medication to ease pain, however.) It has also been reported that the same conditions that influenced the wrong decision of suicide will only have to be re-experienced in the future, until they are mastered. God does not give us challenges that are too difficult to overcome; but, as Jesus, as Saint Francis, as Mohandas Gandhi and others have admonished, we must cultivate a childlike and heartfelt trust in His mercy.

❦ 4 ❧

The Scope of Heaven

It is just not possible to know everything about Heaven, not until, at the very least, one reaches the stage of omniscience. Souls who have reported back from the heaven world state that it extends beyond what they know or comprehend.

Let us consider for a moment just the *physical* universe. It is estimated that there are 100 billion stars just in our Milky Way Galaxy. It is now also estimated, due to recent findings from observations using the Hubble telescope, that there are 10 times the previously believed number of 200 billion galaxies. Therefore, just in the physical universe alone, there are two trillion galaxies that may each contain 100 billion stars. Scientific calculations conclude that there are literally more stars in the heavens than grains of sand on Earth. The extent of just the physical universe is mind-boggling!

When we consider the afterlife, the various levels, planes, or dimensions of vibration *beyond the physical dimension*, we can multiply the possibilities further. For one consciousness to comprehend it all would require an all-knowing consciousness. There have been reports by some people who have had a near-death experience or an out-of-body experience that they were briefly gifted with the feeling of omniscience—of seeing and knowing all. Or, that they were given the "grand tour" of "everything." If this were true, it would obviously still be impossible for them to describe the entirety of what they experienced, of so much vastness. Even if it could be, the number of volumes required to contain the descriptions would surely be endless.

Unfortunately, this book can only provide details about some of the places that we go after leaving physical embodiment, based on various descriptions of the Summerland and areas above and below it. We are clearly not focusing on all the afterlife realms or other life forms, either from the Earth or from countless other worlds; though it is probably safe to say those souls who experience such other realms will likewise experience the fruits of their loving or un-loving choices.

Although various sources confirm the descriptions of the afterlife given in Part II, there are also some books that describe scenarios less beautiful, and sometimes less joyful, or less free. Let us remember that *with God all things are possible*. Since our beliefs and expectations can influence how we live our earthly lives and, therefore, what type of afterlife we may come into, it makes sense to focus on the numerous descriptions of the afterlife that are the most logical, beautiful, loving, and freeing. Given the vast body of testimony from those who have made journeys beyond "death," the underlying direction as one ascends these higher levels or planes is clear.

We now know they are emphatically filled with more Light, Love, Joy, Beauty, and Peace.

❧ 5 ❧

The Afterlife Is *Logical*

ogic would dictate what God, our Creator, would want for His children. We can identify with what we would ideally like for *our* children here on Earth. God, the source of all love, has more love to give His children than parents on Earth are able to give. God has designed life for us to have countless life experiences and has created a loving design for the afterlife for our *maximum happiness!* He has designed our eternal afterlife experience so that we will have:

- *Free Will*—which we have on Earth as well as in the afterlife. We make mistakes and learn from them. We are free to reach our own conclusions about things.

- *Love*—so prevalent in the Summerland levels and higher. Kindness and helpfulness are what everyone practices.

- *Knowledge*—there is constantly more to learn.

- *Purpose*—there are countless occupations and pursuits for our fulfillment and the joy of helping others.

- *Justice*—in the afterlife, we ourselves, from our more spiritually enlightened state, are able to understand and judge our own mistakes, often with the help of more evolved souls. And, if we have fallen short in our Earth life, we may temporarily have to spend time in a "less than ideal" environment—one that is actually of our own making.

- *Honesty*—there is no lying, dishonesty, or corruption—because a soul's thoughts and true intentions are always apparent.

- *Health*—everyone in the Summerland and higher realms enjoys perfect health. There is no need for food or drink, although they can be enjoyed if desired.

- *Financial Freedom*—there are no concerns over money, for there is no need for money. In the afterlife what is important is the joy of selfless, loving service.

- *Comfort*—there is perfect weather in the Summerland and higher realms, with a perfect temperature, so that some souls choose not to have homes because they prefer to live outside.

- *Energy*—an abundance of energy exists for souls to do good works. And, there is no need for sleep, once the initial adjustment period is over. In fact, there is no night.

If this sounds ideal, it's because it is. All of these life conditions are what we would want for our children. And this "holistic paradise" is what Our Loving Father provides for us.

Weigh the evidence alongside the divine logic of it all. Does the evidence demonstrate divine justice? Does it convey ongoing purpose and fulfillment for all? Does it make sense? Do the many different sources usually agree on these main points? Do the most recent discoveries of physics and science confirm that such an ideal state would be possible?

The answer is "YES!" to all these questions!

PART II

DESCRIPTIONS
OF THE AFTERLIFE

❧ 6 ❧

Summerland!

Everyone, at one time or another, dreams of a place, a paradise, where everything is beautiful and everyone is kind and loving. In fact, most of us have probably daydreamed of summer, the most pleasant season of warmth, with sunny and carefree outdoor activities, lasting throughout the year! Well, we are so very blessed, because such a place is waiting for us.

We use the term "Summerland" to refer to this wondrous realm. It has also been referenced by many other names: the "Garden of Eden," the "Third Sphere," the "upper astral plane" and the "lower etheric octave." It is a place that has been described as intermediate between Earth and the true Heaven of the Bible. In other words, in the realms higher than the Summerland, the environment and the souls who abide there are even more beautiful and loving.

There are several different nomenclature systems used by different afterlife sources for the various regions, planes or states of consciousness in the afterlife. Due to the somewhat conflicting and overlapping definitions of the term "Summerland" used by different religions and philosophies, Summerland in this volume is not necessarily identical to the Summerland referred to, for example, by Theosophical or other philosophies, but probably has numerous identical elements.

Additionally, the use of the term "Summerland" in this volume does not necessarily incorporate afterlife aspects associated with the term "Devachan," a place or state of consciousness of "wish fulfillment." Devachan has also been called a "dwelling place of the gods" and a "temporary para-dise." Based on various afterlife reports, the Summerland appears to be relatively more real and permanent than Devachan. Some, but not all, of our sources used the term "Summerland," which was the closest fit from all identification possibilities to use.

This region of perpetual summer encompasses one or more planes or realms between Purgatory and the "True Heaven," which is even more beautiful but more difficult to describe. "Summerland" is used in this book to represent the beautiful environments that many souls describe in their reports from the other side.

The Summerland has been described as a perfect manifestation of form, compared to the Earth with its many imperfections. Sources refer to the happiness, love and beauty that await souls in the Summerland and higher realms. The pleasantries and amenities of the Earth are but a poor copy of what is to come.

7

The Afterlife Is Beautiful

To help keep all the following descriptions in the right perspective, let us first touch briefly on the meaning and purpose of life. Many different answers from many sources have been offered in response to this question. My own research into the commonly-held principles shared by world religions revealed that the meaning and purpose of life is to love, and that our life with God is meant to be good. Joy is the result of a loving life in close communion with God. To experience this natural evolution of increasing joy and love it is our responsibility to do our part in using our God-given free will to practice a heartfelt and loving service to others.

In addition, after extensively researching the afterlife, the preeminent importance of *beauty* became evident to me. According to reports from many different sources there is an incredible degree of beauty in the afterlife. Beauty makes human life more enjoyable, and the beauty of the Summerland surpasses our fondest dreams.

And here we speak of beauty in many forms. There is great beauty in increasing the love in our relationships, and in kind and selfless acts. In addition, the afterlife provides a wonderfully beautiful environment, a beauty that continues to escalate as the "higher realms" are attained.

There are many afterlife books that focus on other aspects of the afterlife, but in my opinion, it is vital to include and establish the beauty that pervades the afterlife and the immense joy this gives to all who come to dwell there. This perspective is a helpful foundation for afterlife studies.

❧ 8 ❦

General Descriptions

There have been many descriptions that have been reported regarding the beautiful and lovely environments in the Summerland and higher realms. Here is another excerpt from H. W. Engholm that provides an overview of the afterlife:

...a Spiritual Universe of unimaginable immensity and grandeur, with sphere upon sphere of the realms of light which stretch away into infinity. We are told that those who have passed from our Earth life inhabit the nearer spheres, amid surroundings not wholly dissimilar from those they have known in this world; that at death we shall enter the sphere for which our spiritual development fits us.[24]

Saint Teresa of Avila (1515–1582) is a Roman Catholic saint. She was a significant contributor to Christian mysticism, and a nun famous for her humility and holiness. She was also a great teacher and led a contemplative life of prayer and meditation. Among her many revelations was this rather stunning observation:

In light of heaven, the worst suffering on Earth, a life full of the most atrocious tortures on Earth, will be seen to be no more serious than one night in an inconvenient hotel.[25]

The mother of Reverend Owen, after she passed, transmitted many telepathic messages to her son, who in the early twentieth century was well respected for his messages from several sources in the afterlife. She described the heavenly realms to her son as being beyond the beauties and wonders one can find in fairy stories. Here are some of her descriptions:

[My home] is beautifully appointed within and without. Within are baths and a music room and apparatus to aid us in registering our work. It is a very large place. I called it a house, but it is really a series of houses, each house allotted to a certain class of work, and progressive as a series. We pass from one to another as we learn all we can from any particular house. But it is all so wonderful that people would neither understand nor believe; so I would rather tell you of the simpler things.

The grounds are very extensive, and all have a kind of relation to the buildings, a kind of responsiveness. For instance, the trees are true trees and grow much as trees do on Earth, but they have a kind of responsiveness to the buildings, and different kinds of trees respond more to one house than to the others, and help the effect and the work for which that particular house was raised. So it is with the grouping of trees in the groves, and the bordering flower beds of the paths, and the arrangement of the streams and falls which are found in different parts of the grounds. All these things have been thought out with marvelous wisdom, and the effect produced is very beautiful.[26]

Reverend Owen's mother also states that her environment is even more wonderful than we could understand, for many of the "wonders" simply have no parallel with our earthly existence. She continues:

The atmosphere... is naturally affected by vegetation and by buildings... those houses have not been raised merely mechanically, but are the outcome—growth, if you will—of the action of the will of those high in rank in these realms, and so of very powerful creative wills.

The atmosphere also has an effect on our clothing, and enters into the influence of our own personalities in its effect on texture and color. So that while, if we were all of the same quality spiritually our clothing would be of the same tint and texture, by reason of the atmospheric influence, this is in fact modified by the degree in which our own characters differ one from another...

The water also is very beautiful. You hear of water-nymphs and suchlike beings in the Earth life. Well, I may tell you that here, at any rate, these things are true. For the whole place is pervaded and interpenetrated with life, and that means with living creatures.[27]

The fact that help comes from higher souls for house building and numerous other "enhancements" demonstrates a great spirit of loving kindness at the higher levels of life. Knowing our Creator cares deeply for each of us, it is not the least surprising that life is abundant everywhere in the heaven world.

And it is very comforting to know that our loving Father wants us to avoid unnecessary stress that would result from changes that are too large or too sudden in the afterlife. Although there are significant differences from life on Earth, souls newly arrived there receive a gradual orientation, so that as the more profound and astonishing aspects of life in Heaven are revealed, awareness and comprehension are developed in such a way that the individual soul can adjust without extreme disorientation or undo shock. In fact, it is reported that souls who have lived an "unprogressive" life on Earth enter into environments that are virtually indistinguishable from Earth. This frequently results in souls not realizing that they have died! Then, gradually, as souls learn and evolve, the character of their environment changes to one of ever-greater beauty.

To better understand what death is all about, it is helpful to keep in mind the nature of God as He is portrayed in virtually all of the religious traditions. He has blessed us with His grand design of a gradual and very individualized progression toward greater love, greater beauty, and greater fulfillment without end. And, God is with us in His omnipresence—in His Oneness in all things through His Kingdom!

Monsignor Benson describes one of his earliest impressions of the natural beauty found in the afterlife:

We walked along until we found... a "pleasant" place beneath the branches of a magnificent tree, whence we overlooked a great tract of the countryside, whose rich verdure undulated before us and stretched far away into the distance. The whole prospect was bathed in glorious celestial sunshine, and I could perceive many houses of varying descriptions picturesquely situated, like my own, among trees and gardens. We threw ourselves down upon the soft turf, and I stretched myself out luxuriously, feeling as though I were lying upon a bed of the finest down.[28]

The beauty of these lands and the beautiful homes for any souls who have earned them are the result of the return of what we give out. "Whatsoever a man soweth, that shall he also reap."[29] These words describe a universal process, and the beauty of the flowers and all of nature is the result of seeds that we plant during our lifetime on Earth.

Some traditions would call this "karma"—the law of cause and effect. Whatever we do, whether it is good or bad, returns to us in some form. It is this law, along with the law of "like attracts like" that results in all souls learning the lessons they need to learn. This is also how we can all be assured that divine justice prevails, and that those who have consciously and intentionally caused great suffering will, in some form or another, have to experience some degree of the emotional and possibly even physical pain they have caused others. Further descriptions of this law of cause and effect will be found throughout this book. The more this fact of human existence is understood, the easier it becomes for a soul to meet challenges and to pass the tests and the trials that are encountered in the world. (More information on this topic is located in the chapters on "Life Review," "Judgment," and "Purgatory and Hell.")

When Monsignor Benson arrived at his spirit home he noticed that it was nearly identical to his home on Earth, with a few differences in the structure that reflected changes he had wanted to make on Earth but never completed. He also noticed that his spirit home had no kitchen, since there was no need or desire for food or its preparation. Houses in the afterlife provide a place of peace and repose, but not a shelter from bad weather, for bad weather simply does not occur!

If you were to take the most perfect summer's day upon Earth that you can recall to your mind, in so far as the weather itself were concerned, you would still be far, far below the splendour of the heavenly summer of these realms. And with us every day is summertime.

Incidentally, we never become tired of it. I have not found one single, solitary individual in these regions who has at any time expressed the wish for a change of weather. When you come here and sample it for yourself, you will feel the same about it, I am certain.[30]

In this beautiful land of perpetual summertime there are no seasons of death or decay—life is in constant and full bloom. Reverend Owen shares the following description:

Trees and plants do not appear for a season, and then die. They bloom perpetually, and then, when plucked, they are fresh for a long time, but they do not droop and wither. They...fade, or melt away into the atmosphere. This same atmosphere is not always white.... It is not a mist, and does not obscure, but bathes all things in its golden radiance without invading the various colors themselves. In other places it is of a faint pink or blue. And every region has its own peculiar tint, or sense, of color, according to the nature of the people and their employment and bent of mind.[31]

Owen continues by reporting about the best aspect of the Summerland; what adds to its beauty beyond all else. And this, of course, is the transcendent, otherworldly love that is shared by all its inhabitants:

As one visits a strange district, one very speedily begins to feel, within and without, that sense of brotherhood and sister-hood, which is one of the most delightful of blessings I have found. Everywhere you go you find brothers and sisters. Try to think of it and see what it would mean if it were thus on Earth. Then the Angels' greeting of Peace and Goodwill indeed would be realized and Earth would be the antechamber of the heavenly Home.[32]

What joy to live where all souls are loving, kind and of good nature, eager to help whenever possible! It is reported that the sense of love in the atmosphere is palatable, and that its true meaning in life is revealed. We can learn from this how important it is for each of us to increase the love in our world, to share it with everyone we know. Since loving is our true nature, and "like attracts like," it is wise, joyful and beautiful to flood our world with greater love. Thereby, we do—truly—create a bit of Heaven on Earth.

The Summerland is continually growing and being im-proved. Its environment is continuing to be created and en-hanced for the benefit of us who will follow. This type of work is just one of countless forms of expression that souls may un-dertake. In a subsequent chapter, "The 'Daily' Activities in the Afterlife," many occupations are described.

❧ 9 ❧

The Transcendant Beauty
of the Afterlife Flowers

It is a joy to find delightful descriptions regarding flowers in the afterlife. Monsignor Benson contributes wonderful detail about their abundance throughout the Summerland. In this excerpt he describes the flowers around his home:

Numbers were to be found, of course, of the old familiar blossoms, but by far the greater number seemed to be something entirely new to my rather small knowledge of flowers. It was not merely the flowers themselves and their unbelievable range of superb colourings that caught my attention, but the vital atmosphere of eternal life that they threw out, as it were, in every direction.

As one approached any particular group of flowers, or even a single bloom, there seemed to pour out great streams of energizing power which uplifted the soul spiritually and gave it strength, while the heavenly perfumes they exhaled were such as no soul clothed in its mantle of flesh has ever experienced. All these flowers were living and breathing, and they were, so my friend informed me, incorruptible.

There was another astonishing feature I noticed when I drew near to them, and that was the sound of music that enveloped them, making such soft harmonies as corresponded exactly and perfectly with the gorgeous colours of the flowers themselves. I am not, I am afraid, sufficiently learned musically, to be able to give you a sound technical explanation of this beautiful phenomenon.... Suffice it for the moment, then, to say that these musical sounds were in precise consonance with all that I had so far seen...and that everywhere there was perfect harmony.[33]

Betty Eadie, in her best-selling book *Embraced by the Light,* describing her near-death experience, also tells of the music produced by flowers—especially one particular rose that captured her attention:

It was gently swaying to faint music, and singing praises to the Lord with sweet tones of its own.... I felt the rose swaying to the music of all the other flowers, and I felt it creating its own music, a melody that perfectly harmonized with the thousands of other roses joining it. I understood that the music in my flower came from its individual parts, that its petals produced their own tones, and that each intelligence within that petal was adding to its perfect notes, each working harmoniously for the overall effect—which was joy.
My joy was absolutely full again! I felt God in the plant, in me, his love pouring into us. We were all one![34]

I suggest that we can now conclude that the term "flower power" is nothing to ridicule! The power of flowers to influence our afterlife environment is tremendous, as they contribute beauty not only to our sight, but also to our sense of hearing and smell, while they touch each soul with their high spiritual and loving energy.

It is reported that by gently holding a flower it is possible to feel life energy from it traveling up your arms. Also, as any particular flower is approached, that flower will bend forward to meet you.

Many of these flowers are not meant to be picked, while others are grown for just that purpose. What would happen if a flower that was not meant to be picked *was* picked? Apparently, no "disastrous calamity" would occur, but the soul who picked it would feel regret. In this heavenly world, there are plenty of blooms available to be picked, and this is often done, where souls take them into their homes just as is done on Earth. It is reported that these picked flowers survive as long as they are appreciated. But when interest in them fades, they rapidly disintegrate, leaving no remains.

Another wonderful characteristic of the innumerable gardens in the afterlife is that they require minimum maintenance. Once a garden is created, the flowers and other plants within it do not undergo the constant decay, winds, storms, droughts or other possible causes of stress that plants on Earth experience. Gardens in the afterlife require practically no attention. What little attention is called for is joyously undertaken by a soul who loves to do that kind of work for the benefit of others, as well as themselves.

Some people might wonder why there are so many flowers in the Summerland—and, specifically, what is their significance? But souls from the afterlife report that the essential reason appears to be the same as on Earth. God has created flowers for our enjoyment, for the wondrous characteristics they provide. They give us in their shapes, colors, scents, radiation and lyrical musical tones ever-deeper experiences of our Creator. Flowers reveal the love that God has for us, His children.

Flowers clearly have a greater influence on the environment in the afterlife than they do here on Earth. Souls can have their senses flooded from the abundance of flowers for their healing, enjoyment of the environment, and sense of well-being and peace.

A high soul named Zabdiel also describes, through the hand of Reverend Owen, the beauty of the flowers in the afterlife:

We see flowers blooming, some of the daisy family, and the pansy, and others standing aloft as if rejoicing in their beauty of foliage and coloring, like the dahlia and the peony and the rose. All these, and more too—for we in this sphere know no flow-ers in their seasons, but all bloom together in the perpetual, but never-wearying summertime.

Then, here and there are other kinds, and some are of great diameter, a veritable galaxy of beauty, like great shields of flashing light, and hues all beautiful, and all giving forth delight to the beholder. The flora of this sphere is beyond description to you, for as I have already explained, there are colors here, which Earth knows not, by reason of its grosser vibrations, and also be-cause the senses of the human body are not enough refined for their perception.[35]

Every flower and every plant is perfect, in full bloom, and given its life energy by our Creator and jointly by all the souls in the afterlife who shower them with admiration and love. All of these plants are created by various spiritual agents of the Creator.

We can appreciate and anticipate a beautiful future environment where we feel so fully attuned and at-one with the astonishing gifts of nature that our Creator has infused into the afterlife. Imagine the profound oneness that is felt and en-joyed between all souls and all plants in the afterlife...including a degree of consciousness and intelligence we could never have imagined. We are all in a tremendous stream of life that flows directly from our loving Creator. Souls directly experi-ence an inherent intelligence within all things.

In this, we witness a confirmation of the work of mod-ern physicists, several of whom have come to endorse the Eastern, and especially Hindu, teaching on the "Web of Life." There is scientific support for their conclusion that at sub-atomic as well as on cosmological scales, all Life, in fact all of Creation, is energetically interconnected. In short, what were once merely viewed as vague if tantalizing assertions by Aris-totle and other Greek philosophers, and intellectually remote assertions by more modern geniuses such as Einstein and Tesla, are becoming twenty-first century science.

God loves His children so very much that He has, with His all-knowing wisdom, created an endless progression of joys, revelations and new forms of existence to share with us. In later chapters, we will investigate the exhilarating and meaningful tasks available to occupy us, as well as abundant forms of enjoyable research, exploration, the arts, and recreation.

❧ 10 ❧

The Astonishing Beauty
of Water in the Afterlife

The glorious environment that awaits us includes water that, like the flowers and plants, has tremendous spiritual healing and energizing power. And, like the flowers, the waters provide color and even music.

Reports indicate that there is an abundance of water in the Summerland with streams, rivers, ponds, and lakes throughout. It is all absolutely pure and not only wonderfully drinkable, but has delightful qualities not found on Earth. It is crystal clear and never stagnant.

In the afterlife, waters in a river, stream, or brook, due to the wondrous qualities of their movement, create beautiful, harmonic musical tones. It is reported that the water appears to be like liquid crystal that reflects light into all the colors of the rainbow. Touching it results in an exhilarating and energizing sensation.

Monsignor Benson, upon reaching a lake, describes his first total immersion in the afterlife waters. He reports it being a spiritual experience:

I discovered that the water felt more like a warm cloak thrown round me than the penetration of liquid. The magnetic effect of the water was of like nature to the brook into which I had thrust my hand, but here the revivifying force enveloped the whole body, pouring new life into it.

It was delightfully warm and completely buoyant. It was possible to stand upright in it, to float upon it, and of course, to sink completely beneath the surface of it without the least discomfort or danger....

That the water was living one could have no doubt. It breathed its very goodness by its contact, and extended its heavenly influence individually to all who came within it. For myself, I experienced a spiritual exaltation, as well as a vital regeneration, to such an extent that I quite forgot my initial hesitancy and the fact that I was fully clothed....

As I emerged the water merely ran away, leaving my clothes just as they were before. It had penetrated the material just as air or atmosphere on Earth will do, but it had left no visible or palpable effect whatever. We and our clothes were perfectly dry![36]

The rivers in the afterlife flow in the same way as those on Earth, starting as small streams and gradually becoming wider and deeper. They have been described as slow-moving and always crystal clear. They contain no merchant vessels and the riverbanks contain no dingy docks in need of repair. Instead, the rivers carry pleasure boats, and their banks are beautiful, not a host of factory buildings but perfectly landscaped dwellings of all sizes. Benson elaborates:

You can have no conception how glorious it is to glide along such a river in some graceful boat, passing through the rolling banks of flowers upon either hand, or through some peaceful meadow where the trees reflect their shapely forms in the tranquil waters; or again, to draw alongside some beautiful broad marble steps, to go ashore, mount to a greater height and view the ribbon of scintillating colour that the river reveals itself to be from this higher elevation; or, yet again, to proceed up some sequestered backwater to find one's self in the midst of a friend's garden.

Nothing can possibly convey to you the brilliance of the

colour, always the colour, that seems to abound in such full measure in the neighbourhood of the rivers. Perhaps it is that the streams themselves reflect back so much colourful light from the flowers that this effect of seeming preponderance of colour is produced. Whatever it may be, we all feel the same about it, and for that reason the rivers always have a very great attraction to the folk in their leisure moments.[37]

Betty Eadie describes the vitality of the water, as well as its intelligence and its music, based upon her near-death experience:

Life. It was in the water too. Each drop from the waterfall had its own intelligence and purpose. A melody of majestic beauty carried from the waterfall and filled the garden, eventually merging with other melodies that I was now only faintly aware of. The music came from the water itself, from its intelligence, and each drop produced its own tone and melody which mingled and interacted with every other sound and strain around it. The water was praising God for its life and joy.[38]

There are seas as well as lakes and rivers. Through the hand of Reverend G. Vale Owen, a spirit guide describes a trip from lakes and streams to the sea:

A plateau is seen stretching away between the shoulders of two hills, and on it rises the chief city of a colony of happy people, who come and look down on us from aloft, and wave their salutation, and throw flowers to us as love tokens.

So we pass along and at length emerge into a valley that opens out on either hand, and very beautiful it is here. Groups of trees cluster about fair and stately mansions, and some, of the more homely kind, of timber and stone; and lakes there are and streams falling with sweet music into the river that runs onward from the mountains round that we have come into the distance before us. Here the valley closes again, and we see two giant pillars of natural rock through which the road must pass side by side with the river.

We emerge through this Gate, which the Valley people call the "Gate of the Sea," and before us we see the open ocean, into which the river falls from a great height, and is very lovely to see as it falls, like many thousands of kingfishers and hummingbirds making their many-colored flight down the mountainside, flashing and sparkling, into the waters below. We descend by pathways and stand on the shore.[39]

Based on reports, the ocean waters in the afterlife include the color reflected from the sky, as well as light reflecting all colors from surface wavelets. There are never strong winds, so the waters remain calm. Beach areas are enjoyed by souls sitting on the shore. The water is always pleasantly warm for swimming and it contains life-enhancing spiritual energies.

It is also reported that the Summerland even has boating available. Apparently, if a soul has earned the right, it is possible to have one's own boat. A boat may have the outward appearance of an earthly yacht with graceful lines, but will be lacking in any visible means of propulsion. Because the power of thought is virtually unlimited in the afterlife, and as we shall see later it provides a soul's means of moving about, thought power can also be used to move objects.

In the afterlife, all things contain a life force. For that reason, all things can be influenced by thought power. So, it is possible for a soul who has practiced this to be able to move even a large boat through the water with only the power of his thought. It is usually not possible for any soul to do this without some understanding of how it is to be done and without concentrated practice.

❧ 11 ❧

The Beautiful Birds
of the Afterlife

In the Summerland, there are many wonderful birds that carry a multitude of colors on their plumage. No birds show any fear for they know that no harm will come to them. Like all life forms there, they do not have to spend their time hunting for food. They sense they are a part of the natural and eternal order of the afterlife, there for their own enjoyment and that of all who are with them.

The mutual trust and good communication existing between souls and birds makes visiting them a beautiful experience. Monsignor Benson describes the mutual love and attunement between them:

It was their trusting friendliness that was so delightful by comparison with the earthly birds, whose life there takes them into another world almost. Here we were part of the same free world, and the understanding between the birds and ourselves was reciprocal. When we spoke to them we felt that they knew just what we were saying, and in some subtle way we seemed to know just what their thoughts were. To call to any particular bird meant that that bird understood, and it came to us....
Why, I asked myself, should the Great Father of Heaven create all the beautiful birds solely for the Earth-plane—and make them to live in places that are frequently quite inaccessible to

man, where he can never see them and enjoy them? And even those that he can see and enjoy are they to perish forever? Would the far greater world of spirit be denied the beautiful things that are given to the Earth world? Here was the answer before and around us. It is in the conceit and self-importance of man that he should think that beauty is expressly created for his pleasure while on Earth.

Incarnate man thinks he has the monopoly of beauty. When he becomes discarnate he eventually wakes up to the fact that he has never really seen how great beauty can be, and he becomes silent and humble, perhaps for the first time in his life![40]

From Reverend Owen a surprising use of birds on the other side is reported—not an essential use, but one simply for the mutual enjoyment of the people as well as the birds. He describes:

...flights of birds coming from out the distance and going, with perfect precision, to some particular spot. Now there are messenger birds trained on Earth, but not as these are trained. In the first place, as they are never killed or ill-used, they have no fear of us. These birds are one of the means we use to send messages from one colony to another.

They are not really necessary, as we have other quicker and more businesslike ways of communication. [But] we use them more as pretty fancies, just as we use colors and ornaments for beauty's sake sometimes. These birds are always making flights, and are dear, loving creatures. They seem to know what their business is, and love to do it.[41]

All the animals in these realms are gentle and harmless. They have no need for food so they have no fear of being prey to one another. Their existence offers souls in the Summerland great joy, and their own joy is evident as well.

❧ 12 ❧

Will We See Our Pets Again?

Many people have had dogs, cats, and other pets who have since passed on. These pets have been sorely missed. Two contemporary afterlife researchers, Roberta Grimes and Bob Olson, each have concluded that we will see our departed pets in the hereafter.

Roberta Grimes, in her book *The Fun of Dying,* reports that the souls of animals will go to one of two places. If an animal dies without having experienced any loving human relationships, without a loving bond to a human, it returns to the "group soul" of its species. If, however, an animal has established a loving relationship with a person, it develops a unique identity. She reports that these loved pets are awaiting our arrival to greet us.[42]

Bob Olson, in his book *Answers About the Afterlife,* not only concludes from his research that we will see our pets again, but that we will be able to easily communicate with them due to the telepathic nature of afterlife communication.[43]

There are, however, definitely mixed views on this subject. Some biblical scholars question whether or not animals have souls. Those who don't believe they do state that animals cannot enter into Heaven for that reason. But it is good to see that there are several biblical passages that support the opposing view. From Revelation:

Behold, I make all things new....
He that overcometh shall inherit all things.[44]

"All things" could very likely include all animals, including our pets. Another Bible verse from St. Luke puts it simply:

And all flesh shall see the salvation of God[45]

Also, some scholars argue that because the Garden of Eden had animals, which was supposed to represent an ideal place, it stands to reason that in the ideal place of Heaven animals also exist. The following quotation from Romans appears to confirm this:

The creature itself also shall be delivered from the bondage of corruption into the glorious liberty of the children of God.[46]

In addition, in 1990 Pope John Paul II weighed in on the subject:

The animals possess a soul and men must love and feel solidarity with our smaller brethren.[47]

The sources chosen for this book contain several references to animals being in the afterlife. Since "With God all things are possible," it would seem very likely that those animals could include our former pets. God loves His children, and would very likely make it possible for us to see our beloved pets again.

☙ 13 ❧

The Lovely Trees
and Surrounding Atmosphere

Trees are an integral part of the beauty of nature, and our sources acknowledged their existence in the afterlife. How could we have all the other lovely aspects of nature and not also have trees? Monsignor Benson tells us how perfect the trees are in the Summerland. He also describes the light in the atmosphere:

> There were many splendid trees to be seen, none of which was malformed, such as one is accustomed to see on Earth, yet there was no suggestion of strict uniformity of pattern. It was simply that each tree was growing under perfect conditions, free from the storms of wind that bend and twist the young branches, and free from the inroads of insect life and many other causes of the misshapenness of earthly trees.
> As with the flowers, so with the trees. They live forever incorruptible, clothed always in their full array of leaves of every shade of green, and forever pouring out life to all those who approach near them.
> I had observed that there did not appear to be what we should commonly call shade beneath the trees, and yet there did not appear to be any glaring sun. It seemed to be that there was a radiance of light that penetrated into every corner, and yet there was no hint of flatness.

My friend told me that all light proceeded directly from the Giver of all light, and that this light was Divine life itself, and that it bathed and illumined the whole of the spirit world where lived those who had eyes spiritually to see.

I noticed, too, that a comfortable warmth pervaded every inch of space, a warmth perfectly even and as perfectly sustained. The air had a stillness; yet there were gentle perfume-laden breezes—the truest zephyrs—that in no way altered the delightful balminess of the temperature.[48]

❦ 14 ❧

The Perfectly Delightful Buildings and Habitations

The types of architecture and the building materials used in the Summerland add to our overall understanding of what it's like there. The goal is to only have buildings that are beautiful. It is reported that there is a wide variety of architectural styles that represent the very best from the past to the present, the Gothic style being one of the favorite styles used. Souls who originally designed buildings in various past eras in Earth's history enjoy recreating their best works.

The materials used are significantly more beautiful than those used in Earth structures, for they radiate delicate colors and some can be partially translucent. In addition, their coloring and texture can change somewhat in response to souls in their vicinity. All the colors are harmonious with their surroundings and with other buildings in their area.

It is interesting to note what type of architecture is *not* appreciated for its beauty. It is reported that thin and plain-looking buildings are not considered beautiful and therefore do not exist. There are no long rows of identical-looking buildings. Any structure that is not considered beautiful by its inhabitants would simply not last long. Only buildings that are loved and appreciated for their appearance and functionality exist in the afterlife—otherwise they just literally fade away.

Reverend Owen describes building possibilities and comments on how long buildings last. His description is from the perspective of someone being able to look down upon the various buildings to observe their surroundings:

He would see all around him dwellings and buildings of various kinds.... But those buildings would not be merely houses and workplaces and colleges to him. From each structure he would read not its character so much as the character of those who built it and those who inhabit it.

Permanent they are, but not of the same dull permanency as those of Earth. They can be developed and modified and adapted, in color, shape and material, according as the need should require. They would not have to be pulled down, and then the material used in rebuilding. The material would be dealt with as the building stood. Time has no effect on our buildings. They do not crumble or decay. Their durability depends simply on the wills of their masters, and, so long as these will, the building stands, and then is altered as they will.[49]

The actual "ownership" of a building is determined not by how much was paid. In the spirit world the only right of ownership is the spiritual right, which is determined by the sort of life we have lived upon Earth, as well as whatever progress has been made since entering the afterlife.

We will learn more about "spiritual right living" as we continue on to more aspects of the afterlife. In general, this involves loving kindness as the default standard of personal behavior in the afterlife. Right living involves practicing the Golden Rule and feeling love and gratitude toward our Creator for everything including the joy of loving relationships.

⚜ 15 ⚜

The Afterlife Is Far More Real and Tangible than Life on Earth!

Modern science has demonstrated that ultimately all matter is composed of energy. It has been established that the universe is an interconnected and interwoven energy field—and energy at the quantum level cannot be destroyed, it can only change form. From this foundation of knowledge about matter, it is not difficult to conceive that the Earth, as well as all levels in the afterlife—really everything in the universe—was brought into form by the thoughts of our Creator. All sentient life forms, to a greater or lesser degree, are co-created with the energy and the intelligence of God.

In the afterlife, thought is far more tangible and its effects are far more immediately evident. Souls have a clarity of thought that yields a far greater sense of reality. This is because a soul's thought processes are not shrouded or impeded by the physical brain.

To the souls abiding there, the Summerland appears just as solid as the Earth. This may be hard to believe, because here on Earth we haven't fully realized this power of thought. Because of the difference in vibratory levels between the Earth and the afterlife, souls who have made their transition and then return to visit the Earth will find nothing solid for them— walls can easily be passed through. If seen by someone on

Earth, souls would appear unsubstantial, if visible at all. (Souls on a positive and purposed mission back to Earth usually have attained the ability to lower their vibratory rate so that they can be seen, if required.)

And the afterlife levels are invisible to nearly everyone on Earth. The sense of reality, and what feels solid, is a relative thing. Having our consciousness free from the confines and limitations of the physical body and being closer to the spiritual source of all life makes for a greater sense of reality.

This clear sense of greater reality is evident in the Summerland. Some souls, however, when first arriving in the afterlife, arrive in lower levels of the astral plane, where they initially experience less reality in the form of dreams and illusions. These "dream experiences" are often closely associated with a soul's very recent experiences and relationships on Earth.

It is possible that "ultimate" reality may not include anything material. Many equate the term "reality" with physically solid things...but ultimately reality could very likely be a consciousness aware of the creation process of all things. No matter how "real" any object or place seems, it is still the product of its spiritual and mental source.

A description of all relevant states of existence, of all possible realms of consciousness, is way beyond the scope of this book. In fact, we may humbly state that given the likelihood that God's creation is, quite literally, infinite and without end, no book, or library of books, could ever completely describe all the possible levels of existence and consciousness.

For now, we are primarily focusing on the Summerland and areas in close proximity to it. Various sources state that life there looks and feels more real than Earth life. A highly evolved soul communicating through Reverend G. Vale Owen put it this way:

The body you now wear, and the trees and rivers and other of material substance, which you call real, are not so enduring, nor so real, as their counterparts in these spheres. For here is found the energy which comes to your systems, and is as the electric dynamo to the single lamp as to its power and intensity.

When, therefore, men think of us as whiffs of smoke, and of our environment as drifting shadows, let them pause and ask if there is any sound reason to bottom [support] their view. Nay, there is no reason in it whatsoever, but, on the contrary part, it is foolishness.[50]

Monsignor Benson points out that many need to shed their view that the afterlife environment is a wispy and nebulous realm. Here he explains his reasons for providing so much detail about the afterlife (and a number of researchers agree that Benson's reports provide greater detail about certain afterlife subjects than anyone else):

To wave aside such particulars as I am giving you because they seem trivial and very earthly and unworthy of consideration when 'heaven' is under discussion, is to hold a totally wrong conception of spirit lands. We are live people living in a beautiful land, a land far more solid than the Earth. We love the countryside and the city; we love our houses and gardens, we are blessed with delightful friends. But the country and the city; the houses and the gardens, and, lastly, our friends have more substance about them than can be found upon Earth, and this substance is made up of such details as I am describing to you.[51]

After sufficient time is spent in the Summerland, it is reported that a soul will yearn for the greater reality and beauty of what lies beyond, in higher realms. These levels are described in several accounts as being more subjective and less objective—"physical" items and environments may be more fluid and changeable—more spiritual and less physical. This does not make them any less real, however.

Dr. David Fontana is the past president of the Society for Psychical Research, professor of transpersonal psychology at Liverpool John Moores University, and author of numerous best-selling books. In his book *Life Beyond Death*, he affirms his belief that once an individual soul reaches a point where they long for a more real and permanent environment, they will move to higher levels that are closer to the spiritual source of all reality:

All these thought-created environments are by their nature temporary. Once the soul realizes this it begins to long for the permanent behind the temporary, the real behind the illusory, and once all opportunities for spiritual development in the Plane of Colour [thought-created environments] have been satisfied, it is ready to move on to the higher non-illusory levels.[52]

This subject of what is ultimate reality has been dealt with at length by scientists, cosmologists and religious scholars. Perhaps the Bible says it best in this simple observation from Corinthians:

For now we see through a glass, darkly; but then face to face: now I know in part, but then shall I know even as also I am known.[53]

The time of experiencing ultimate reality is well beyond our immediate future. After we make our transition most souls will have the opportunity to enjoy the earthlike beauty of the Summerland.

❧ 16 ❧

The Spiritual Body

There are several bodies that interpenetrate [to penetrate between, within] the physical body. Each of these various bodies vibrates at different rates—all higher than the rate of the physical body. Our physical body is influenced by these layers of vibrating energy, and each of these layers or bodies has its own particular purpose.

These bodies, especially those with vibration rates closest to the physical body, form a matrix or template for our physical body. These "subtle" bodies establish an interconnected field of energy within and around the physical body. Each subtle body links into the physical body via chakras, which are concentrated spheres of energy. In addition, electro-magnetic energy moves through our central nervous system and out through meridians that connect all the organs and systems of the physical body, and even extend as electro-magnetic fields, in many cases, several feet beyond our physical forms. Most of what is stated here is confirmed through modern, science-based studies in the fields of naturopathic medicine, acupuncture, and Kirlian photography.

Each of the subtle bodies has an "aura" that cannot be seen by most people in the physical except by those who have developed their psychic abilities. These select individuals are able to view the faster vibration rates of one or more of these higher bodies surrounding the physical form.

There are different schools of thought pertaining to the order and naming of these higher bodies. Some schools call the next higher body the "etheric" while others call it the "astral." Beyond those, most agree that there is an "emotional" body, a "mental" body (sometimes divided into "lower" and "higher" levels), and a "causal" body. For our purposes, there is little need to use these names. Suffice it to say that our physical body is able to be formed and is influenced by these various invisible and more subtle bodies that interpenetrate it.

We have certain hints as to what life will be like without a physical body. When we dream, we are often aware that we have some sort of body, often one that resembles our earthly form, though a more "light-weight" version. Those who have had near-death experiences and others who have had out-of-body experiences frequently report an awareness of their spiritual body.

Rudolph Steiner, in his book *Theosophy*, and using his choice of terms for the various bodies, lists them as follows:

The physical body as the coarsest structure lies within others that mutually interpenetrate it and each other. The ether body fills the physical body as a life-form. The soul body (astral shape) can be perceived extending beyond this on all sides. Beyond this, again, extends the sentient soul, and then the intellectual soul, which grows the larger the more of the true and the good it receives into itself.[54]

Robert Crookall, in his analysis of decades of descriptions of the afterlife, believes along with several others that our physical "death" is merely the first of several "unveilings," each of which results progressively in more harmonious environments. According to Crookall, after physical death, we operate for a brief time from the soul body plus the "vehicle of vitality" (some refer to this as the "etheric double"). During this time, any conscious experience we may have is dreamy or "sub-normal" and we are in an illusory environment. After this usually brief time Crookall says we undergo a "Second Death," which consists of the shedding of the "vehicle of vitality" from the soul body. Once this has been shed, the soul body is enabled to experience a higher state of consciousness than was possible while in physical embodiment. We can then enter the "Paradise State" which he defines as:

> ...the normal 'next' world of the average and above-average 'dead.' The Soul Body corresponds to this environment. It is 'semi-physical' and is not the 'super-physical' true 'Heavens' of the Bible (which is entered after the 'Third Death,' i.e., the shedding of the Soul Body).[55]

Crookall defines the "Third Death" as the shedding of the soul body at the end of the "Paradise State," when the "True Heavens" (higher realms) are entered. Once this attainment has been achieved "mystical or cosmic experiences" can occur:

> There is a third 'death'—that transition in which the Soul Body itself is discarded. After this event, consciousness operates at Spiritual 'levels' in the Spiritual or Celestial Body, with the indescribable true 'Heavens' as the environment. The third 'death,' more properly described as the third unveiling of the Greater Self, leaves no 'corpse,' 'husk' or 'shell' (as do the first and second): in this process the body undergoes a progressive refinement and purification and consequently an increase in responsiveness. It is mentioned here only to complete the correspondence envisaged between the succession of bodies, 'levels' of consciousness and environments.[56]

According to Crookall, when souls leave the Summerland level for higher levels, the "soul body" will be shed. What souls look like then depends not only on their individuality, but which of the several sources of information about these higher realms are accurate. It is not necessary to know now what our ultimate appearance will be like once we have transcended these more known realms of the afterlife to come into environments more beautiful and different than can be described.

Let's return to Monsignor Benson for a description of what it is like to be in a "spirit body"—in Paradise conditions, or Summerland. His use of the term "spirit body" probably refers to the "soul body" in Crookall's terms:

The spirit body is, broadly speaking, the counterpart of our earthly bodies. When we come into the spirit world we are recognizably ourselves. But we leave behind us all our physical disabilities. We have our full complement of limbs, our sight and our hearing; in fact, all our senses are fully functioning. Indeed, the five senses, as we know them upon Earth, become many degrees more acute when we are discarnate. Any supernormal or subnormal conditions of the physical body, such as excessive stoutness or leanness, vanish when we arrive in these realms, and we appear as we should have appeared on Earth had not a variety of earthly reasons caused us to be otherwise.

There is a stage in our lives on Earth, which we know as the prime of life. It is towards this that we all move. Those of us who are old or elderly when we pass into spirit will return to our prime-of-life period. Others who are young will advance towards that period. And we all preserve our natural characteristics; they never leave us. But we find that many minor physical features that we can profitably dispense with, we shake off with our earthly bodies.[57]

There exist many forces on Earth that cause imperfection in form, including stress, accidents, and illness. Fortunately, none of these exist in the Summerland or higher realms. Like the perfect well-formed trees in the afterlife, the bodies that a soul utilizes in these realms are more perfect than the one we used on Earth. They require no care or maintenance—as described earlier, they are always in good health.

No physical malnutrition can occur, but in the lower levels of the astral dimension, "spiritual malnutrition" can occur. Spiritual bodies are nourished from many sources, all part of the one flow of life from our Creator. Spiritual force, or energy, is one of the main components of the air that souls breathe. The light in the atmosphere provides another source of energy, as well as the color in it. Energy is also obtained from the flowers and the water, as previously described, and from the sheer joy of being amidst beauty in all directions. Last but not least, energy is received directly from our loving Father, who blesses us with a constant flow of "magnetic current," as it has been described, which is constantly charging our spiritual bodies with life force.

All of these forces surround the spiritual body of every soul. No effort need be made to seek these forces out, in stark contrast to life on Earth, where we must daily obtain our food and drink. No effort is required of a spiritual body to eat, digest, and assimilate food that is taken in. It is impossible to block this continual flow of divine life!

What does it feel like to be a "spirit person?" We learn that the soul no longer has to experience fatigue, hunger, thirst, disease, accidents, or stress! Even though the soul's body feels so much lighter, it is yet possible to feel like a virtual giant, with a fully alert mind. The soul experiences a feeling of supreme well-being and vitality. There are no feelings of being too cold or too hot, or any other discomfort. Everything in the environment of the Summerland and higher realms is perfectly adjusted to the souls who live there—the temperature, the dwellings, the land, the rivers, the lakes and the entire landscape. Most important of all, the inhabitants dwell in love and harmony with one another. All of this presents an environment where unhappiness cannot exist.

As referenced in the previous chapter, matter is ultimately vibration. But what can this literally mean? The higher soul, Zabdiel, through the hand of Reverend Owen, gives us some insight, relating this to the makeup of our spiritual bodies:

Matter itself is the result of the transmutation of spiritual vibrations into those of grosser sort, and these latter are now being analyzed by scientists who have come to the knowledge that matter is indeed the result of vibrations, and that no article of matter is still, but in ceaseless movement. That is correct, but not conclusive, for it does not pursue the matter to the end of it. It were truer to say, not that matter is in vibration, but that matter is vibration, the result of vibration of a quality more refined, which is found, not in the phenomenon of material things, but in those [higher] spheres proper to its quality.

Thus you will see how little it matters that, when the time comes for you to cast off the body of Earth, you stand discarnate. Your Earth body was a body of vibrations and no more. Very well, you now have a body of vibrations more substantial and enduring, because of a higher quality, and nearer to the energizing Will which brought it into existence, and so sustains it. That body will serve you while you sojourn in the lower spheres and, when you have progressed, that body will be transmuted into one still more permanent, and of quality more sublime. This process will be repeated as the ages go by and you proceed from glory to higher glory in the infinite reaches of progress before you.[58]

We know from quantum physics that our bodies and all things physical are ultimately vibration. This is confirmed in numerous quantum experiments involving sub-atomic particles, the "stuff" that comprises all of matter. Our human mind can perhaps only begin to grasp this incredible physical phenomenon.

❧ 17 ❧

Clothing in Summerland

B ased on different afterlife sources, it appears that souls can wear any type of clothing desired. It is reported that the clothing can be altered at will. Souls wear what they wore while on Earth when they first arrive. After a time, they usually choose to blend in with the various robes often worn by souls in residence. If there is an occasion, however, for a soul to appear to family and friends who have recently arrived, or the rarer instance of appearing to them on Earth, familiar Earth clothing is worn to help them be recognized as they formerly appeared on Earth.

According to Gladys L. Hargis, the author of *You Live Forever*, a soul can be in a lower level (such as Purgatory, discussed in a subsequent chapter) where souls wear robes that are gray. After passing through a white light everything is cleansed and their robes become brilliantly white.[59]

In Betty Eadie's *Embraced by the Light,* she describes a group of souls in a garden, many who were wearing "soft pastel gowns." She also mentions a tour of a beautiful room where many souls, both male and female, were busy weaving on "large, ancient-looking looms."

They were anxious for me to see the workmanship of their hands. I went closer and picked up a piece of the cloth that they were weaving. Its appearance was like a mixture of spun glass

and spun sugar. As I moved the cloth back and forth, it shim-
mered and sparkled. Almost as though it were alive.... The work-
ers explained that the material would be made into clothing for
those coming into the spirit world from Earth.[60]

Other sources claim that merely by wishing or desiring to change one's garments the earthly style of clothes can be discarded through the simple process of having them just fade away and immediately replaced by one's own unique spirit robe. The robe's color and the intensity of the color are dependent upon the individual. It is reported that most people embrace the change, as their earthly clothing seems quite drab compared to the more colorful afterlife garments and environments there.

Robes in the afterlife can be rather varied, and there are usually at least some differences between the color and shape of one soul's robe and those of another. It is reported that many beautiful tones and shades of color are possible from the robes, because they hang in multiple folds about the wearer. They are also described as being extremely comfortable and staying in perfect condition.

Monsignor Benson describes what he has seen to be worn about the waist, the feet, and the head, and explains that spiritual adornments are earned:

Many people will be found wearing a girdle or sash
around the waist. Sometimes these will be of [a cloth] material;
sometimes they appear to be of gold or silver lace.... In all cases
of the latter, they are rewards for services performed. No possible
conception can be formed of the superlative brilliance of the
golden or silver girdles that are worn by the great personages
from the higher realms. They are usually adorned with the most
beautiful of precious stones, fashioned in various shapes, and
mounted in beautifully wrought settings, according to the rulings
that govern such matters. The higher beings, too, will be seen to
be wearing the most magnificent diadems [head wreathes] as
brilliant as their girdles. The same law applies to these. Those of

us of lesser degree may perhaps be wearing some such embel-
lishment as I have just described, but in a greatly modified form.

There is an enormous wealth of spirit lore behind the
whole subject of spirit adornments, but one fact can be plainly
stated: all such adornments must be earned. Rewards are given
only upon merit.

We may wear what we like upon our feet, and most of us
prefer to wear a covering of some sort. It usually takes the form
of a light shoe or sandal. I have seen numbers of people here who
have a predilection for going barefooted, and they do so. It is per-
fectly in order, and it excites no comment whatever. It is natural
and commonplace with us....

We seldom wear any covering upon our heads. I do not
remember seeing anything of the sort anywhere in this realm. We
have no need for protection against the elements![61]

Whether we don clothing made by our brothers and sisters, or merely think of and visualize what we'd like to wear,
we will be well attired. Our ultimate clothing may merely be
our light-bodies radiating the light of our Divine Presence.

⚜ 18 ⚜

Mobility Using Thought

Regarding mobility, numerous reports indicate that a soul in the Summerland level or higher can quickly learn to travel from place to place by using the power of thought. There are certain restrictions in this movement, however, as a soul would not be able to travel to significantly higher vibratory levels without assistance. At first, traveling to lower vibratory levels would be done with assistance as well, for the proper purpose and with precautions. Proper etiquette would also be followed, where a soul would not choose to suddenly appear without good cause to inappropriately interrupt other souls.

Souls can choose whether or not they want to walk or actually teleport themselves instantly. Teleporting requires confidence, which comes quickly after the first successful move. Concentration of thought is required—with full concentration, one simply wishes where they want to be. Conscious effort is required the first few times, then it becomes automatic—just as on Earth when we decide to get out of a chair and walk, we don't have to think about the details of all the movements required to make it happen.

This method is simple and natural. Remember that the soul body is extremely light, and the spirit world is a world where thought has evident power. Basically, when one thinks, one is taking action. This thought-action is instantaneous.

Once this method of transportation is practiced a few times, it becomes second nature. It is still quite enjoyable, however, for souls to simply walk from place to place.

❧ **19** ❧

Inspiration from Higher Realms

The power and presence of light and love are more prevalent and more intense as one ascends through the higher levels of Summerland and beyond, compared to the lower levels of the astral. To be clear, there are degrees of light and love flowing to all dimensions throughout the universe. And all souls are nourished by this light and love, though in varying degrees.

Julia Ames, through the hand of William T. Stead describes her realization in the afterlife:

The greatest, the most delightful, the only important thing, compared with which all other things are as nothing, is that by what you call Death we have come into a far closer, more intimate realization of His presence, of His Life in us, and our Life in Him.[62]

Although souls in the afterlife levels enjoy serving their fellow brothers and sisters, they evolve at different rates due to their individual thinking and previous life experiences. Several sources point out that there exist no religious creeds to follow, there is only the loving kindness of mutual help encompassed by the Golden Rule.

Individual souls can benefit from the occasional uplifting of their spirit from ceremonies they participate in, which include visits from one or more higher souls who descend to their level radiating great light, love, and wisdom. These are times when souls focus on their goals with deep thought and intensity. They enjoy sharing these occasional ceremonies with each other, as well as with higher souls. Such ceremonies are said to help dissolve blocks in the consciousness, which then allows more light to enter in.

From his place in the Summerland, Monsignor Benson described a visit from a higher soul, who came bestowing upon them new levels of inspiration, guidance and power. He relates that they were blessed not only with the visitor's own radiance, but the radiance of the higher heavenly sphere from which he came...

Before our eyes, there appeared first a light, which might almost be described as dazzling, but as we concentrated our gaze upon it we immediately became attuned to it, and we felt no sensation of spiritual discomfort. In point of fact—as I discovered later—the light really became attuned to us; that is to say, it was toned down to accord with ourselves and our realm. It grew in shade to a golden hue upon the extremities, gradually brightening towards the center. And in the center there slowly took shape the form of our visitor. As it gained in density we could see that he was a man whose appearance was that of youth—spiritual youth—but we knew that he carried with him to an unimaginable degree the three comprehensive and all-sufficing attributes of Wisdom, Knowledge, and Purity.

His countenance shone with transcendental beauty; his hair was of gold, while round his head was a lustrous diadem. His raiment was of the most gossamer-like quality, and it consisted of a pure white robe bordered with a deep band of gold, while from his shoulders there hung a mantle of the richest cerulean blue, which was fastened upon his breast with a great pink pearl. His movements were majestic as he raised his arms and sent forth a blessing upon us all. We remained standing and silent while our thoughts ascended to Him Who sent us such a glorious being. We sent our thanks and we sent our petitions.[63]

Sister Frances Banks describes the benefits and joy of one such ceremony that included the presence of a soul from higher realms:

One is conscious of a supreme quickening of tempo, a heightening of the action of the dynamo of the Spirit. There is a distinct feeling of growth; the body seems to expand, to become less gross, to stretch into a new elasticity and ethereal content. The mind soars to a hitherto unexplored vastness of creative activity. The Spirit fills all with a dynamic lift of consciousness. New and vast concepts stream into the mind. The onward Path is illumined with a clarity that surpasses all imagination.[64]

These ceremonies will certainly act as the ultimate "life coach" and be of tremendous assistance to every soul. How wonderful it will be to have the occasional energizing inspiration and road map of the next steps along life's journey. The ceremonies are also opportunities for giving thanks for the many joys of life and spiritual evolution.

There are higher, more beautiful and loving environments that souls aspire to after adequately experiencing the Summerland level. There is good and useful work available to be done in all these dimensions, as well as ever-increasing levels of peace, joy, love and harmony.

❧ 20 ❧

Newly Arrived Souls
Often Need Rest

The type of experience newly arrived souls have after their transition from Earth life depends on their previous life experience. Souls who are aware of at least some of the fundamentals of the afterlife and who die a natural death arrive at their appropriate location without needing any rest. Many souls are in shock, however, due to either a violent passing, or after a painful and protracted illness. These souls need special attention before they can move forward in their new environment.

We learn from souls in Summerland that there are those dedicated to helping the newly arrived who need extra care. They assist them to come to an understanding that they have "died," and they acquaint them gradually with their new world. There are homes specially designed for this where orientation can best take place. Reverend Owen's mother, residing in spirit, comments on one such home that specializes in helping souls who have undergone great stress:

We hope to be able to tell you a little more of the love and blessedness which we experience in these bright realms. Our Home is situated on the slope of a thickly-wooded hill in a clearing, and our "patients"—for they are really such—are tended by

us here in peace and quiet after their distressing experiences....
They come here more or less exhausted and weak, and are only
allowed to go onward when they have become strong enough for
the way.[65]

Monsignor Benson described one of the homes of rest
as having a powerful shaft of blue light descending upon it and
infusing it with special qualities. This light contained soul-
healing energy:

An outer vestibule led into a lofty hall of considerable di-
mensions. The space that would ordinarily be devoted to win-
dows was occupied by tall pillars set some distance apart, and
this arrangement was carried out through all four walls.... The
floor was carpeted with some very soft covering in a sober design,
and here and there a handsomely wrought tapestry was hanging
upon the walls.
Occupying the whole of the floor space were extremely
comfortable-looking couches, each of which bore a recumbent
form, quite still, and obviously sleeping profoundly. Moving qui-
etly about were a number of men and women intent upon watch-
ing the different couches and their burdens.
I noticed as soon as we entered this hall that we came
under the influence of the blue ray, and its effect was one of pro-
nounced energizing as well as tranquility.... Those in attendance
upon the sleepers did so, not in the attitude of a certain task to
be done willy-nilly, but as though they were performing a labor
of love in the sheer joy of doing it. Such, indeed, was precisely
the case. The glad awakening of these sleeping souls was an ever-
recurrent joy to them, no less than to the people who had come
to witness it.[66]

One section of a home of rest is described as being
filled with souls who had experienced lengthy illnesses before
making their transition. Immediately after they leave their
physical bodies they are gently sent into a deep sleep. Due to
their prolonged illness, their minds can suffer a temporary
weakening, and this can temporarily affect the soul at a deep

level. The best course of action is to ensure that the individual soul has the chance for a complete rest and a complete orientation—the amount of time depending on the individual's needs.

Many souls who awaken from their sleep do not realize that they have "died." Those who have been watching these souls and are waiting for their awakening then have a great task to perform—successfully getting the news across to the soul that they have left their life on Earth—and doing so in the gentlest way possible. Just prior to the soul's awakening, their loved ones in the afterlife convene to help them realize their new circumstances.

If these souls had been more informed about some of the basics of the afterlife, they might have spared themselves significant stress. Far too many people decide to "wait until they get there" before they learn anything about what is in store for them. Especially difficult to deal with are those who have never believed in life after death. These souls often need a lot of assistance in grasping the essentials of the afterlife.

For those who have had a violent or sudden death, upon awakening there can be significant confusion, as it appears to them there has been no break in their lives. These souls receive especially loving attention until they are convinced and adequately comforted concerning what has happened to them.

It is reported that souls who know little to nothing about the afterlife are extremely sensitive to the tiniest details in their initial observations. It is logical and natural for them to be concerned about where they are and what others are like. For such reasons, it's extremely important for the soul's "caretakers" to act relaxed and natural. They can terrify a newly arrived soul if they act too serious, grave or grim. Benson remarks upon the importance of how these caretakers appear to new souls and how small details matter:

In the initial moments of the newly arrived, so much depends upon the little incidents, those homely things, of great implication in themselves, and outwardly so very reassuring and comforting.

Long experience has taught us that often the smallest, most insignificant incident can do far more to bring peace and mental quietude to the newcomer to spirit lands than would a hundred of the most brilliant dissertations. Therefore, it is that we deliberately introduce the apparently trivial.[67]

In other words, caretaking soul workers do everything possible to assure the newly arrived that there is nothing to be concerned about. Rather, that the new place of existence that they are entering is truly a blessing, not something to fear, but a wonderful future to look forward to.

❦ 21 ❧

The Soul Undergoes
a Life Review

During the life review, souls see and often actually experience a detailed replay, in chronological order, of their earthly actions and interactions with others, the important choices they made, and even significant thoughts that occupied them during their life on Earth. They also are able to experience how their actions affected others by actually feeling what those others felt. Souls witness their most secret thoughts, feelings and motivations, which may have been repressed or simply forgotten.

Howard Storm, in his book *My Descent into Death*, described a life review during his near-death experience. He was asked if he'd like to see a summary of his life and he agreed. He states he was with Jesus and seven angels or saints, and that the review was their objective record rather than what he necessarily remembered about his Earth life to that point. "They reported the thoughts and feelings of people I had interacted with..."[68]

It has been reported that some souls experience two separate life reviews—one that is purely objective without all the accompanying feelings and another where all the feelings of both the soul and those interacted with can be felt. Some souls apparently require two life reviews while others do not, depending on the lives they led and their degree of soul development.

An advanced Being, or any number of higher souls may be present during this review, providing the soul with an atmosphere of total acceptance and absolute, unconditional love. The review gives the soul an opportunity to witness and to take responsibility for all their actions from their Earth life. Only then can the soul go forward by addressing mistakes that were made and realizing what needs to be done before moving on.

Life reviews frequently commence right after the question is posed to the newly arrived soul, "What did you do with your life?" After the review, the real motives of the soul are made clear, and then a "judgment" of the soul (addressed in a following chapter) can occur.

In many cases these reviews are disappointing, as frequently there are two contrasting descriptions that come into the consciousness—one being the "divine blueprint" for the life to be lived, specifically the plan that was created before embodiment for the soul to accomplish the most growth and do the most good. The other description is a recording that shows what actually happened in that lifetime. Obviously, the differences can be huge, resulting in major disappointment. The experience can be a shock and truly humbling: to discover so little was accomplished when such great opportunities presented themselves. Sometimes souls are too guilt-ridden, timid, or frightened to face the necessary work alone, and this requires extensive help.

Some souls, witnessing in their life reviews all the suffering they have caused, actually become immobilized after their life review. Other more mature souls are made available to help the distressed individual reach the point of wanting to make amends for their failures and the hurt they have done to others. These souls receive a variety of caring techniques by which they gradually make amends and thereby rise above and leave behind the mistakes, difficulties, and the harms done while on Earth. It has been reported that souls who need extraordinary help are allowed to see their life review again, more slowly and in reverse, starting from the moment of death and slowly going backward, accompanied by a high soul who provides needed wisdom and support during the process.

Dannion Brinkley is an internationally known author whose early life included successful sniper missions and other forms of violence before experiencing a deadly lightning strike and a temporary but soul-transforming visit to the afterlife. His two astounding near-death experiences are described in his best-selling book, *Saved by the Light*. Brinkley came to believe there was great value in the life reviews he experienced. It allowed him to examine his life objectively, without any ego involvement.

In his second book, *At Peace in the Light,* Brinkley analyzes his near-death experiences, and reports that without ego and also with the increased empathy he felt during the life review, he was enabled to make a "totally honest appraisal of all the aspects of my life."[69] He believes the value of the life review makes for far better life decisions afterward. He also stated:

An examined life is certainly a far richer one. By putting everything else aside and reflecting on our lives from a spiritual point of view, we see ways in which we could have performed better in the past and will perform better in the future.[70]

The fact that people sometimes experience life reviews during near-death experiences, as well as after their final transition into the afterlife, demonstrates that there really are no secrets. Our Creator, in what is surely great mercy, provides the soul a review so the individual can reform, make amends and grow ever more in God's Light.

🌿 22 🌿

Motive Is All-Important

W hen we understand the wonderful future that awaits us in the afterlife, we will naturally feel a joyful anticipation for when that time arrives. However, this joyful anticipation, while wonderful, is not meant to be the *main motive* or intent for our helping others and doing good works. Radiating love to others, often in the form of serving others, is the *true nature* of our being. The *simple joy of helping others,* once all else is cleared away, is the divine spark behind our motivation to do good. This is our pure and natural motivation, our primary and most powerful motivation—more important than any anticipation of receiving any other rewards that await our good works. This may appear to be a subtle difference in our motivation, but it is an important one.

Again, the motivation behind souls who help others through kindness and service is the simple and basic pleasure they experience while doing so. For that reason the type of "work" a soul in the afterlife chooses is often the same as what the soul had chosen to do while on Earth, where they had become expert in its performance. Under afterlife conditions, their actions are far easier to perform, and the joy is magnified, without any thought of reward other than the immediate pleasurable feeling while the task is accomplished. The wish to assist others is always the highest and first desire.

Stafford Betty in his book, *The Afterlife Unveiled*, offers his view of proper motive:

Sometimes a skeptic will say that if we knew what to expect in the afterlife as a reward for virtue in this life, we would do the right thing for the wrong reason—for a selfish reason. That's not the way it feels to me. If I do the right thing, I do it because it is right. Believing that there is some sort of karmic reward for doing it only makes it easier to do. It doesn't determine me to do it; it merely adds incentive to do it.[71]

Professor Betty also cites the example of Mother Teresa, who practiced a long and difficult life of selfless service not for reward, but for her "clarity of vision," and because she had a giving heart. She could simply see that it was the "right thing to do."

Monsignor Benson reports visiting a "Hall of Literature," which had one of its many large sections devoted to history. There, Earth's true history is revealed. What amazed him was that alongside the reporting of the facts that actually happened were very revealing statements of motive:

I found that side by side with the statements of pure fact of every act by persons of historical note, by statesmen in whose hands was the government of their countries, by kings who were at the head of those same countries, side by side with such statements was the blunt naked truth of each and every motive governing or underlying their numerous acts—the truth beyond disputation. Many of such motives were elevated, many, many of them were bitterly base; many were misconstrued, many distorted.

Written indelibly upon these spirit annals were the true narratives of thousands upon thousands of human beings, who, whilst upon their early journey, had been active participants in the affairs of their country. Some were victims to others' treachery and baseness; some were the cause or origin of that treachery and baseness. None was spared, none omitted. It was all there for all to see—the truth, with nothing extenuated, nothing suppressed. These records had no respect for persons, whether it be king or commoner, churchman or layman.... It required no adornment, no commentary. It spoke for itself.[72]

This addresses the difference between appearances and intent. It drives home the point that nothing can be hidden, that why we do what we do comprises our true character, and this is how our measure is taken in the world of spirit.

What really counts in our earthly lives is the motive behind our deeds. Our motives may be of the highest, but the actual deed may have a poor external appearance. And the reverse is equally true. For example, a man may give vast sums of money for some charitable purpose with the sole thought of personal publicity and self-aggrandizement. While the gift itself may do great good to those upon whom it is bestowed, the motive behind the gift will not be to the giver's spiritual advantage. But if this same donor were to perform a small service to another person in difficulty or similar circumstances, all not witnessed by a third party, and with the sole intention of helping a fellow mortal in distress, such unobtrusive and stealthy service brings a rich reward to him who performs it. It is motive, always, that counts.[73]

❧ 23 ❧

Judgment

One of the most important and powerful verses in the Bible (equivalent statements can be found in the sacred texts of other world religions) is found in Galatians:

Be not deceived; God is not mocked: for whatsoever a man soweth, that shall he also reap.

For he that soweth to his flesh shall of the flesh reap corruption; but he that soweth to the Spirit shall of the Spirit reap life everlasting.

And let us not be weary in well doing: for in due season we shall reap, if we faint not.[74]

These three verses contain a powerful truth. If we practice acts of goodness and kindness to our brethren, we will be blessed in the same way. If we focus solely on gratification of the flesh, and not of the spirit, we will find ourselves in the afterlife with lingering desires of the flesh that cannot be fulfilled, and we will feel deficient in spiritual light. If we persevere in doing our good works, with faith and determination, even under extreme hardship and various challenges, our goodness will attract goodness back to us.

Many people who report on their near-death experiences recall having a life review and agreed that they were the ones who judged themselves. We do this from a place of higher wisdom—not only is our consciousness freed from the clouding effect of the confining human brain, but—more importantly, we work from our "Higher Self."

The Higher Self is the part of every soul that is eternal, divine, and one with the "Christ Self," the Christ being the one son of God, the intermediary between God and man...as opposed to the lower self which is associated with ego and imperfection.

The Higher/Divine Self that we each have is what connects us all with God and each other. This concept of a higher aspect of our human identity is, in various ways, confirmed in all of the world's major religious traditions. Much more information about the Higher Self can be found on Google, in numerous other spiritual books, and in my previous book, *Unifying Truths of the World's Religions*.

During the process of our soul's judgment, we receive guidance regarding what we can do to make amends for our errors, in the form of prayers, sending helpful and healing thoughts to those we have harmed, or taking more direct action if it is possible. There are often higher souls who are visible or who remain invisible to assist in guiding this judgment experience.

Some afterlife sources state that we receive guidance from one or several masters that can be viewed as a panel of spiritual judges, a type of "Karmic Board." The degree of karmic board involvement could very likely depend on the level of spiritual attainment (the ability to attune with one's Higher, Christ Self) the soul has reached; souls having a higher level of attainment would require less guidance than a soul with less spiritual attainment. The point is that we experience a life review and use higher wisdom from our own Higher Self along with the help of other higher souls, as needed. In this way, we determine not only how to make amends for our errors, but where to go and what to do next.

It is also worth mentioning that some afterlife sources say that souls just go automatically to their appropriate afterlife destination, without any apparent judgment or assistance from higher souls. If that happens, it may be due to such souls departing their human life in a highly evolved spiritual state.

Sister Frances Banks describes the help available for newly arrived souls as being very flexible, depending on the soul's reactions to the "shock" of experiencing their life review. Many souls need time to adjust and are encouraged to visualize an improving future after they address mistakes made while on Earth.

The newcomers are then introduced to the idea of an expanding progress and are encouraged to right the wrongs they have done in their earth lives by concentrated thoughts of forgiveness and compassion.[75]

Many people believe that once they leave the Earth, they will face a judgment that will lead to significant and possibly eternal punishment. The mother of Reverend Owen states that love is the guiding principle in all the work in the afterlife. She tells of a Mother Angel addressing a frightened soul who first spent some time in Purgatory (see the next chapter for a description of Purgatory) before ascending to a higher plane:

The Mother replied, "My child, your judgment will take place whenever you desire; and from your own words I can tell you that it has already begun. For you own that your past life is

*worthy of punishment, and that is the first step in your judgment.
As to the Judge, well, she is here; for you yourself are judge, and
will mete out to yourself your punishment. You will do this of your
own free will by reviewing all the life you have lived and, as you
bravely own up [to] one sin after another, so you will progress.*

*"Much of your punishment you have already inflicted upon
yourself in those dark regions from which you have lately come.
That punishment, indeed, was dreadful. But that is past and over,
and what you have now to endure will be dreadful no longer. All
dread should now be past. Painful, deeply painful, I fear it will
be. But all through you will feel that He is leading you, and this
more and more as you go on in the right way."*[76]

From this we are reminded that our "punishment" is the
pain we will feel—emotional pain in its many forms, including
guilt, sorrow, and shame for causing the suffering of others.
Souls also feel deep regret over lost opportunities. Souls in the
afterlife will sooner or later come face to face with an awareness of the pain they have caused others. They must be able
to empathize with those who have been harmed—to feel the
emotional pain (and in some cases the physical pain) they experienced. Souls are then enabled to more accurately feel and
know what is right and what causes pain. They are also clearer
in their ability to feel their natural love for others and desire
to help others.

This form of feedback for our accidental or intentional
errors or "sins" makes much more sense than burning eternally in Hell. It also reflects the true loving nature of our Creator: that of mercy and compassion, rather than punishment
and damnation. From feedback or "returning karma" we grow
and learn, developing our ability to love and empathize with
our fellow brothers and sisters. From Reverend Owen we
learn:

*This is what perplexes many who come over here. They
expect to find all [is] set [and] ready for their dismissal from the*

Presence into torture, and cannot understand things as they are.

Others who have cultivated a good opinion of their deserts [rewards] are much disappointed when they are given a lowly place, sometimes a very lowly one, and not ushered immediately into the Presence of the Enthroned Christ to be hailed with His "Well done." Oh, believe me, dear son, there are many surprises awaiting those who come over here, some of a very joyful kind, and others the reverse.[77]

Monsignor Benson also believes that we are our own judges, based on how we have decided to use our God-given free will during our lifetime.

Man, himself, is his own judge. His thoughts, his words, and his deeds, registered upon his mind, are his only judge, and according to how his earthly life has been lived, so will his place be in these lands of the spirit world. This is another natural law, and like all the laws of the spirit world, perfect in its operation. It requires no interpreters of it, no exponents of it. It is self-acting and incorruptible, and, what is most important, it is impartial and infallible.[78]

Many different sources agree that we are our own judge. Once we have an expanded consciousness and are attuned to our Higher Self, we are able to evaluate what we did with our lives on Earth. We will know according to our innate higher guidance what prayers, thoughts of forgiveness, and other acts of amends are possible and called for to help correct the harm done to others. We will experience levels of deep anguish, remorse and sorrow, as our truly loving and divine nature faces the reality of things done on Earth, whether in ignorance or on purpose, that caused suffering for others. (Even acts done intentionally to hurt others—requiring greater amends—are ultimately done through ignorance—a type of ignoring, that is, of spiritual law and our true nature.) We will strive mightily to purify our thought and feeling habits so that we can advance into higher levels where darkness cannot abide. And we will be helped as needed and as we may request, by high and loving souls, and by the blessed, pervasive atmosphere of love and beauty in our new world.

Let us now take a brief look at the lower levels of the afterlife. We may or may not have to spend a limited amount of time at these levels, depending on how we live our life on Earth.

❧ 24 ❧

The Netherworld of Purgatory and Hell

Souls who have been predominantly cruel to others during their life on Earth will spend their initial time in the afterlife, after the process of their life review and judgment, in what is known, according to various traditions, as either "Purgatory" or "Hell." The time they spend there, before they are able to move to higher levels, is dependent on their own free-will cooperation, as well as the degree of wrong behavior they engaged in while on Earth.

Before souls can rise from these lower levels, a "purgation" or cleansing must take place. Significantly, at least a portion of the cleansing process consists of the soul actually systematically experiencing a tangible measure of the actual suffering they have caused others.

The individual soul thereby is most often able to develop empathy for the souls that have been harmed. They will experience deep regret, sadness, and other forms of emotional pain in their realization, coming from their own inner true divine self. They will gain a deeper understanding of the real wrongs they have committed and, mercifully, they will come to recognize their motives and the personal psychology that led them to their unfortunate and hurtful conduct.

By the laws of God and the natural world, only good works accomplished by the soul will offset the wrongs committed. Through all of this the soul comes to understand that these often-hard lessons are the result of a loving Creator extending every possible consideration to the individual and his onward evolution. The soul realizes both the justice and the mercy involved in this process of purgation.

The soul comes to appreciate the divine logic and the inherent goodness requiring the development of genuine compassion and greater wisdom before a soul can enter the higher dimensions of the afterlife.

Purgatory is defined as an intermediate state after physical death, where souls undergo purification, so as to achieve the holiness necessary to enter the joy of Heaven. Some sources state that a significant percentage of souls need to spend at least a small amount of time in Purgatory after their transition from Earth.

Professor Stafford Betty describes Purgatory as follows:

Purgatory is, after all, a process, not a final end. It is a place, a world, where spirits purge themselves of bad habits and tendencies and repent their mistakes.[79]

It is logical that the good and joyous levels of the afterlife, which are inhabited by souls who no longer harbor negative or evil thoughts or intentions, cannot allow souls to be there who still harbor those thoughts or motives. Besides, we know that in these levels no one can lie or pretend—the purity or impurity of the soul is there for all to see. Therefore, a time and a place are necessary for souls to be purged.

Professor Betty goes on to explain that unnecessary suffering or some type of endless punishment for the sins or wrongdoing of an individual does not fit in with:

...an all-wise, all-loving God who desires nothing so much as that we should freely turn toward the good, the beautiful, and the true as we work to uncover our native splendor, so long imprisoned in one body after another, whether fleshly or astral or subtle.[80]

It is the loving nature of our Father/Mother God (for indeed, our Loving Creator has a universal nature that includes a love for His/Her children that surpasses the fondest love that any mother on Earth has for her child) that would not allow us to suffer unnecessarily. Any suffering we experience is necessary to prepare us to be able to enter the beauty of higher realms free of any temptations or urges that would not belong there, that would, in fact, literally bar us from being there in the first place. In addition, it is worth pondering this question: "How can we fully appreciate joy—unless we first experience sorrow?"

The law of the universe, "like attracts like," applies in determining where a soul goes after death. The soul of Sir Francis Bacon, through medium Dr. George T. Dexter, is reported to have stated the following about souls who find themselves in the lower and darker spheres:

The great law of like attracting like obtains throughout the whole of the spheres. When a departed spirit enters into the spheres, he is at once attracted where he finds congeniality of place and persons. [A troubled or less evolved soul] ...could not be happy in the bright spheres. They could find no enjoyment where there is either virtue or goodness. Thus their first efforts are to locate themselves where the acquired attributes of mind in all its workings may be gratified. Their bodies are gross and their minds still grosser.[81]

Souls naturally go to a place that they are familiar with, with other "like-minded" souls. Fortunately, there is another universal law, the "Law of Progress," which reveals the nature of the universe as uplifting. In other words, souls will "see the light" at some future time, even if it takes a very long time.

They eventually realize they can raise themselves up and enjoy greater and more uplifting realms, and then are motivated to set that goal and make the needed effort to get there.

Regarding "Hell," several sources report that the concept of eternal damnation was invented by man to frighten people into correct action. Eternally burning in Hell is a concept utterly alien to the loving and merciful nature of God. Theologians and academicians who have devoted years to the study of sacred scripture have developed a wide variety of theories regarding the biblical concept of Hell. They have essentially proven that there exist several places in scripture where, in the early centuries after Christ, words and whole passages were inserted into and, in other cases, removed from the Bible as we know it today.

The very process of the formulation of the Bible is still controversial today, but there is unquestionable confirmation that a major degree of its modern makeup is the result of a Roman emperor. At the Council of Nicaea in 325 A.D., Roman Emperor Constantine, a military dictator, "decided" via a carefully selected council of religious leaders, which books of the Bible would be included thereafter in his version of Christianity, and which other numerous texts would be excluded. Many scholarly analyses have been put forward on this Council, even up to the present day. The conclusion is that the excluded books make it clear that extremely controversial concepts such as a fiery "Hell" and "eternal damnation," as well as such teachings as women being excluded from the clergy and being "subservient" and "lower" than men were in fact not a part of the true teachings of Jesus. In fact, they were additions inserted for the purposes of control.

In the afterlife, certain spheres are at the lowest levels of the astral plane, and they are indeed extremely unpleasant and even horrific, but souls would not be stuck there for eternity. Of the thousands of varying but credible near-death experiences that have been recorded, not a single one describes a place of endless "imprisonment" and eternal suffering.

According to Attorney Victor Zammit, author of the widely acclaimed book, *A Lawyer Presents the Evidence for the Afterlife*:

> *Those who were consistently cruel are either left alone or are met by those others of the same very low vibrations, with the same very low spirituality to be attracted to the darker lower spheres.*[82]

Most people would find being completely alone very difficult. But being in the presence of those who are consistently malicious and cruel would certainly be even more trying and unpleasant. Experiencing this would definitely result in the soul "getting a taste of their own medicine," and eventually the development of a sense of empathy for others. This is divine justice in action, and it is automatic, due to the law of attraction. Properly understood, this "magnetic attraction" is simply an aspect of karma, the law of cause and effect.

High souls, through the hand of Reverend G. Vale Owen, confirm this necessary experience of suffering in this statement about "Hell."

> *They who, having lived their lives on Earth unrighteously, go by natural attraction downward into the places where they most will benefit by their environment. These you call the Hells. Well, such they be, my son, if hell means anguish and torment and soul-rending remorse.*[83]

Souls need to experience deep remorse for their cruelties to others, and the natural action of divine justice is continually and precisely modulated, until the soul fully and deeply appreciates the needed lesson. What is required of all souls is to transcend their ignorance of spiritual law, to learn about God's divine spirit residing within them, and then apply it in their lives. This may require self-forgiveness first, and certainly forgiveness of others, so that the emergence of a loving heart will no longer be blocked by non-forgiveness, as is so often the case in our earthly lives.

There is always hope and profound assistance available to souls who find themselves in these lower realms. Sister Francis Banks talks about visiting these regions, and the help that is available:

I have visited the 'lower regions' though, I assure you, with Conductors who were able to guide and protect us. Believe me it is a terrible region, or regions, of semi-gloom, of unwholesome 'sticky' emotions, of utter distortion of all that is beautiful. One's feelings are wrung by the pitiful sights; compassion flows out for those poor half-alive creatures in their self-darkness.

There are wonderful Helpers in these regions. These have to be advanced souls, strong in themselves and firm in the Light before they can choose to do such work.[84]

Although there is always help available, helpers must often play a very long "waiting game," for any particular soul to reach a point of accepting responsibility for their wrong-doing and realizing there is hope for an improved future. Receiving helpful guidance depends on how open a soul is to receive it.

Banks affirms the falsity of man's belief in eternal fire and goes on to describe the realities of Hell:

There are hells of the spirit and the mind, confining states of misery; dark, depressing and as real as the tortured consciousness of the dweller therein makes them. Yet these hells are not eternal. The man (or woman) in these mental torments need stay there no longer than his desires keep him. He is free to resist the hatreds, cruelties, lusts of his lower nature, which he has retained from his Earth life and which are keeping him in dark dungeons amid like-minded inhabitants.[85]

The level of remorse can be overwhelming for many souls caught in the lower regions of Purgatory and Hell. Certain souls, by their own free will, choose to be saturated with guilt, gloom and regret. Although they need to feel these things as they develop their sense of empathy—because of the suffering they caused others—they must still be open to progressing beyond that. Sometimes their sadness and remorse are so great that it blocks them from the light that would illuminate them, which would free them from their guilt and show them the way to climb out of the hole they are in.

It is reassuring that by the mercy and grace of God, souls in Purgatory and Hell can always decide to focus on and follow the Light. Higher souls are always available to assist, comfort and guide those who request help.

What of definitive evildoers, those who stubbornly and willfully do evil, and refuse to relent? There are two schools of thought that emerge from a study of afterlife communications and writings. One school holds that all souls can be saved, that sooner or later in the eternal timeframe of the afterlife, the blighted soul can eventually come to terms with the horrific records in its past, work to balance the mountain of misdeeds and traumas incurred upon others, and finally journey back to a loving Father, as did the Prodigal Son in Jesus' parable.

The other school incorporates a modified version: that *nearly all* souls can be saved, but that there are exceptions. In the case of Hitler, for example, and other souls who have truly turned against God and refuse to ever reform or turn away from their evil doings, the soul creates such overwhelming mountains of karma, so vast an amount that it is too great a burden to free themselves from it. Furthermore, the soul is so infused with the "blackness" of its deeds, that essentially not the least spark of light remains as a point from which to even begin to feel any sense of remorse, or to summon any desire to reform and seek the Light. In these cases, it is believed that through God's loving mercy, that particular soul would be relieved of his overwhelming darkness and his energies returned to the ethers.

Leaving that dismal and rare situation, Sister Banks adds hope for reducing the suffering of mankind while on

Earth, with the realization of the power of the mind and the knowledge of our eternal ever-brightening future. She reassures us that progress is just as satisfying in the afterlife as any feeling of success on Earth:

> *One has only to have a glimpse of the Planes of Mind, where emotions have been conquered and transmuted into aspiration, to realize the wonder of Creation and the Love of God for His creatures. One has only to see the dark misery of the self-imprisonment of souls in the shadow-worlds to understand the justice and the balance of the Life Force.*
>
> *When telepathy and mind-communication become more widespread in the world, then will Light be raised up in man and he will realize his oneness with all.*[86]

According to Sister Banks, the time will come when true peace and goodwill on Earth will be possible. People will finally come to understand their God-given gifts, the power of positive thought, the voice of conscience, and the innate compassion placed within the human heart. These gifts lie at the foundation of our nature and animate the human soul. Then, truly, God's Divine Light will shine more brightly on Earth.

❧ 25 ❧

Reincarnation—Do We Return to Earth?

T he subject of reincarnation will not be addressed at length, as it is too controversial a topic. An entire book would need to be written to properly cover its various aspects.

The Abrahamic religions, consisting of traditional Christian, Jewish, and Muslim doctrine teach that there is only a single incarnation. However, from their origins to the present era, groups within these religions do believe in reincarnation. Early Christian teachings acknowledged reincarnation, but they were excluded from the Christian Bible in 325 AD at the Council of Nicaea. Some scholars point to references in the Bible that allude to it. Essentially, all of the Eastern religions, including Hinduism, Buddhism, Sikhism, and Jainism, acknowledge reincarnation.

In addition, early Greek philosophers such as Plato and Socrates taught reincarnation. It is found in the spiritual teachings of Theosophy, the Rosicrucians, the Celtic Druids, as well as Unity Church. And certain American Indian tribes also believe in reincarnation.

Numerous writers, philosophers, and psychologists are also in this company, including Emerson, Thoreau, William

James, Carl Jung, and Nietzsche. There are, no doubt, numerous other notables not mentioned here who are open to the possibility of reincarnation.

Many who have had near-death experiences report reincarnation as a part of our life cycle. Quite a few sources claim that souls do not immediately return to their next life. Instead, long periods can sometimes be spent in the afterlife in preparation for the next embodiment.

Also, there are numerous, highly credible accounts of young children remembering past lives. These children were able to describe people, places and events that they apparently could not have otherwise known. There are several fascinating books on this subject, including *Children's Past Lives* by Carol Bowman; *Many Lives, Many Masters,* by Brian Weiss M.D.; and *The Boy Who Knew Too Much*, by Cathy Byrd.

Most adherents of reincarnation agree that the goal is to perfect ourselves sufficiently so that it is no longer necessary to re-embody. Sufficient spiritual attainment or insights need to be realized before "liberation" from the wheel of rebirth on Earth can be achieved. It is believed that living a righteous life, and including certain spiritual practices such as yoga, meditation, prayer, and fasting could contribute to a soul no longer having to reincarnate.

Reincarnation could help to explain how a soul can live a very brief life in physical embodiment and then be forced to leave its body due to a childhood illness, or due to an abortion. Reincarnation is often explained as being the "mercy of God," which gives us numerous chances to experience life...to learn what we need to learn and to accomplish our unique missions.

Whether or not reincarnation is true, what is important is how we live *this* life. There has to be a good reason, if reincarnation is real, why we have a "veil of forgetfulness" regarding our past lives. One reason would be that it would enable us to start with a clean slate and not be distracted by emotions (such as possible pride or guilt) concerning our past embodiments that would not further our advancement. Hopefully, we would be able to remember, at least intuitively within our heart or within our subconscious mind, important lessons to help us lead better lives toward greater goodness.

26

Soul Groups

After the life review and judgment, the soul experiences an increase in the sense of oneness and empathy with others, and a greater degree of interest in their needs. Our individuality is developed within groups of souls who have interests similar to our own. These groups are sometimes referred to as "group souls." Within them, the wisdom, the strength, and the experiences of each soul in the group are shared with all members.

In these afterlife groupings, souls feel free to express themselves creatively. Because they are in the company of other souls of similar temperament and kind, there is less hesitancy to express thoughts and feelings. Souls can at last present themselves as they truly are, experiencing a most glorious feeling of freedom in their group environment!

Dr. Robert Newton was a hypnotherapist who came to believe in reincarnation after taking clients into deep hypnosis sessions in which they frequently referred to their afterlife experiences before they were born. In his book, *Journey of Souls,* he refers to the "cluster groups" that a soul returns to, and states that the soul is usually "overwhelmed with pleasure" when this occurs, being greeted by familiar souls or "classmates." He also states that the "criteria for group admission is based upon knowledge and a given developmental level."

After physical death, a soul's journey back home ends with debarkation into the space reserved for their own colony, as long as they are not a very young soul or isolated for other reasons.... The souls represented in these cluster groups are intimate old friends who have about the same awareness level.[87]

Doctor Newton also stated that his subjects under hypnosis describe a soul cluster group as containing a small primary number of souls that frequently interact, similar to families on Earth...who also have a much greater sensitivity to each other than family members on Earth. And there are also secondary groups that act as support groups.

Sister Frances Banks addresses the concern that some may have of being just a cog in a wheel, or just one cell in a large conglomeration of cells—in other words, of not having a life as a unique individual. She asks "Why not?" and points out that it is simply not true that anyone's life is isolated from the rest of life, which doesn't mean we cannot create our unique contributions to it. Banks states that:

The whole of nature expresses the unity of the Life Plan, plants, animals, minerals belong to different families, and respond uniformly to prescribed patterns. Should the human then be so different?[88]

Afterlife sources point out that souls are often members of many groups, that there are groups within groups, and all the groups comprise one Great Soul. These usually include groups of families as well as many more that comprise mutual interests. These groups can be actively helping others, in addition to devoting time to studies. Some of the more powerful groups are guided by great souls who understand the divine light in every atom, and where a oneness is experienced with all souls. There are numerous narratives to the effect that members in these higher groups can spark ideas within researchers on Earth that promote helpful innovations that will assist mankind.

Frederic Myers, one of the co-founders in the nineteenth century of the Society for Psychical Research, passed away in 1901. Dr. Stafford Betty, in his excellent book, *The Afterlife Unveiled*, cites communications from Myers years after his death through the hand of Geraldine Cummins, "one of the most gifted mediums of the twentieth century." Myers reported souls in afterlife groups as being a "number of souls all bound together by one spirit," a sort of super-consciousness which inspired all those in the group. Each group could contain anywhere from twenty up to a thousand souls. Myers described a unifying interest that held the group together and which significantly accelerated the progress of its individual members:

The interesting feature of my state here is that I am within a larger mind, and many of my affinities are contained in it.... How fine and beautiful is this brotherhood within the one being; how it deepens and intensifies existence; how it destroys the cold selfishness so necessary to an Earth life.[89]

To the degree that the above description is true, the more highly evolved souls who lead these "group souls" would naturally be focused on what is best for the souls within the group. To those of us on Earth, this sounds like much trust would be required, and perhaps caution flags might be raised. When looking at all these different aspects of the afterlife, we can see that it is designed by God's great love for His children. It is safe to say that the purity, goodness, and trustworthiness of the higher souls who lead these groups is unquestionable. Once we arrive on the other side this will probably be much more evident.

Numerous sources acknowledge these various soul groupings in the afterlife. Once again, we see the law of "like attracts like" in action. When souls are *not* alike, when they lack significant degrees of mutual interest, then there exists little to attract the souls to each other. Each individual becomes detached and goes off to explore other attachments and interests, reflecting the dynamics of relationships on Earth. Some mutual interest has to be present, even if that interest falls short of affection. Even when there is no mutual interest between two souls, however, there is always the understood bond of mutual love of God and an awareness that we are all children of God.

Civility and respect are common denominators among all souls in the Summerland. Even total strangers will be most kind and loving when they interact. If they don't share any mutual interests, they are not likely to go out of their way to get together. Still, the atmosphere and exchanges are mutually uplifting. In addition, whenever a soul temporarily does not desire any socialization, this desire is also readily sensed and the temporary need for privacy is perfectly accepted and honored. Benson addresses this as follows:

Here in spirit we need no formal introductions; we constitute one large united gathering in the matter of ordinary social intercourse. After we have been here a little while, and become accustomed to our new environment and mode of living, we find that we never intrude since we can read at once the mind of a person who wishes for a period of seclusion. And when we see people out in the open—in garden or countryside—we are always welcome to approach and hold friendly converse with them.[90]

Emanuel Swedenborg (1688–1772), an eighteenth-century Swedish inventor and scientist, claimed to have had his spiritual eyes opened and to be able to freely visit Heaven and Hell in the last twenty-eight years of his life. He wrote about souls having similar interests being more attracted to each other, expressing himself in a manner that reflects the age of his work:

Those of like character are brought together as it were spontaneously; for with their like, they are as with their own relations [family], and at home; but with others, as with strangers and abroad. When they are with their like, they are also in their freedom, and thence in every delight of life.[91]

Swedenborg goes on to address soul groups in some detail. He refers to souls in the afterlife as "angels."

It was said above that there are larger and smaller societies in the heavens; the larger consist of myriads of angels, the smaller of some thousands, and the least of some hundreds. There are some also who live apart, as it were in separate houses and families; these, although they live so dispersed, are still arranged in like manner as those who live in societies; that is, the wiser of them are in the midst, and the more simple in the boundaries....
Every society is a heaven in a less form, and every angel in the least, because the good of love and faith is what makes heaven; and this good is in every society of heaven, and in every angel of the society.[92]

As souls evolve, they will change their relationship with a particular group, and at some point may leave the group for higher levels of activity. Whenever souls move on, group members will join in celebrating with the soul in recognition of their advancement. And souls who do leave a group are free to return for visits to tell of their new adventures, which all enjoy.

Within the company of one's soul group, one may express their ideas with no fear of being considered foolish. Because others are not intolerant to a soul's view, that soul has no desire to be intolerant to others. This is not difficult because souls dwell in a happy community with others who are most loving and friendly, showing respect for one another. The many beauties of the environment stimulate the mind and bring out only the very best in everyone. There is no stress caused by the necessity of work or health maintenance. There is nothing that disturbs souls in this environment. Anything that was in a soul that was not his highest and best is simply shut out by the abundance of friendliness and kindness in this atmosphere, similar to the sun on a flower's bloom.

Finally, the following excerpt by Monsignor Benson illustrates how beautiful the quality of life is in the Summerland and higher realms. This is a helpful introduction to the next chapter, which focuses on what souls do with their time:

We have everything that will bring us contentment. Our true natures thrive and expand upon such glories and splendours as the spirit world alone has to offer. We work, not for an earthly subsistence, but for the joy that comes with doing work that is both useful and congenial, and above all things, work that is of service to our fellow beings. The reward which the work brings with it is not a transient reward as is the case with so much mundane labour, but a reward that will bring us eventually to a higher state of living.

To us here in the spirit world, life is pleasure, always pleasure. We work hard, and sometimes long, but that work is pleasure to us. We have not the tiresome wearying toil that you have upon Earth. We are not solitary beings fighting for our existence amid a world that can be, and so often is somewhat indifferent to our struggles. Here in these realms wherein I live, there is not one solitary individual of whatever nationality under the sun who would not come immediately to the assistance of any one of us upon the merest glimmering of our needing help. And such help it is! There is no false pride that precludes our accepting help from a fellow creature anxious to give it.

Millions of us though there be, yet there is not one sign, not one atom of discord to be seen throughout the immense extent of these realms. Unity and concord [agreement] are two of the plainest characteristics to be observed and understood and appreciated to the full.[93]

⁓ 27 ⁓

The "Daily" Activities in the Afterlife

O nce a soul has gone through all the initial steps upon entering the afterlife, including grand and wonderful reunions and exchanges of news with "predeceased" friends and relatives, the point is reached where "what to do" takes center stage. It is extensively reported that no person still in embodiment can possibly conceive of all the various types of useful and interesting work there is to do in the afterlife. Compared to living on Earth, where it is necessary to earn a living, provide nourishment for the physical body, as well as a roof over head, and attend to numerous other relatively burdensome tasks, the afterlife soul is freed from all those necessities.

The kind of life a soul led on Earth largely determines the quality of residence and the type of clothing the soul will have, as well as the quality of their environment. But there is no physical necessity to work in the afterlife. The term "work" is used here because of no ready replacement. What a soul does in the afterlife is mostly quite enjoyable. In the Summerland and higher realms, everyone "works" because it is so fulfilling to do things that others need or enjoy. Imagine how beautiful a life this is. All glory to God!

There are many occupations on Earth that are irrelevant in the afterlife. All the souls who had jobs on Earth that are no longer needed will soon come to that realization. However, to offset that, they will of course quickly realize they have no need to work for food, clothing, or shelter. This results in their immediate sense of a grand new freedom to engage in new and fascinating lines of work. They soon discover exciting and elevating interests and will then join with others in joyfully learning new occupations.

The high soul known as Astriel, through the hand of Reverend G. Vale Owen, makes a fascinating statement about work in the afterlife:

Be sure, friend—and tell others who will hear it—that this life which awaits you is not a mere bodiless dream in a twilight region somewhere beyond the boundary of the real and actual. No; it is strenuous and intense, this life of ours. It is filled with service and endeavors crowned, one after another, with success; of patient pressing onward, and of indomitable wills attuned each to other in comrade service for the Lord of Love, Whose Life we sense and inspire.[94]

According to Emanuel Swedenborg, there are so many offices and administrations and various occupations in the afterlife that it would not be possible to enumerate them. All souls are delighted with their work because it is specifically useful, and they love performing their unique responsibilities. Furthermore, no one works for material gain since everything needed or wanted is freely available. There is no fear of ill health or of becoming exhausted. Souls are free to attune to their true divine nature—the joy of giving and of selfless service.

There are societies whose employments consist in taking care of infants; there are other societies whose employments are to instruct and educate them as they grow up; there are others who in like manner instruct and educate boys and girls who are of a good disposition from education in the world [Earth], and who thence come into heaven; others who teach the simple good from the Christian world, and lead them to the way of heaven; others who perform the same office for the various Gentile nations; others who defend novitiate [novice] spirits—those who have recently come from the world—from infestations by evil spirits; some also who are attendant on those in the lower earth; and some who are present with those in hell, and restrain them from tormenting each other beyond the prescribed limits....

Civil affairs are administered by those who, while in the world, loved their country and its general good in preference to their own, and did what is just and right from the love of justice and rectitude. Such men possess capacity for administering offices in heaven....

The offices which they administer correspond exactly to the degree of their intelligence, and their intelligence is then in like degree also with their love of use for the general good.[95]

One important and rewarding line of work is the treatment of those who awaken from their physical death. Few souls enter the afterlife with much knowledge about it. Consequently, many souls upon arrival need care to get started to overcome their stressed and perplexed state of consciousness. This type of service appeals to ministers of different religious denominations. Ministers realize they are all just a part of one great ministry, sharing the same awareness of what afterlife living is all about.

In these "Halls of Rest" are also doctors and nurses able to help souls that have passed after a long and painful illness. These healing practitioners are also able to help those who have experienced a violent passing. It is reported that there are special schools in the afterlife to teach those that desire to help in this way. Subjects include working with the spirit body, the spirit mind, and an overview of what spirit life is like so they will be able to answer the many questions from these newly arrived souls.

Some of our "telepathic writing" sources have been involved to some degree in the care of these newly arrived souls, which is why they are such good sources due to their keeping close to those with Earth ties. Because the souls who work in this field are properly trained, they are able to provide the best care and guidance to the newly arrived, who can of course be extremely fragile and fearful.

Work requires energy, and that energy is supplied by our divine and unlimited source. It continuously flows through all souls in the measures required, and if a need for greater energy to do a special task is required, it is given. Souls have no need for sleep, except for those who require it upon their initial arrival to the afterlife.

Fatigue occasionally occurs, not as a depletion of energy, but simply from a soul's desire to change from the type of work being done. Similar to life on Earth, a soul can tire of an occupation and want a change of scene or activity. Fortunately, there are said to be endless opportunities for shifting to a new line of work and type of service. And it is possible to switch back to a former occupation. This all occurs in perfect harmony with what is needed and the soul's needs for change and growth.

Bob Olson, author of *Answers About the Afterlife*, states that many souls have communicated that there are schools in the afterlife that teach classes on spiritual growth. He also lists some of the "jobs" in the afterlife:

Some people in spirit help the newly crossed over, while others help with specific circumstances, such as sudden death, suicides, mass murders, or child deaths. There are even people who work with the spirits of animals that cross over.... These... are more like callings that provide us with fulfillment, understanding, and spiritual growth....
We might choose to serve as someone's spirit guide. We might act as a counselor, helping people in spirit process their last life. We might even coordinate coincidences for people on the physical plane to help guide them toward the experiences they preplanned for their life. The possibilities are almost as endless

as the spirit world itself, which means there is one thing that doesn't exist in the afterlife—boredom.[96]

Dr. David Fontana, in his book *Is There an Afterlife?* states that many afterlife sources confirm that learning is available in the arts and sciences for souls who choose to take the path of wisdom. He also mentions a few specific occupations, including helping those who are dying make their transition, sending creative ideas to people on Earth, and sending messages through mediums about the afterlife. His research indicates that there are an unlimited number of ways that have value for souls to assist in a constantly evolving universe.

Dr. Fontana also concludes that communicators from the afterlife want to assure us that the afterlife is *not* boring, and that it is *not* merely "full of celestial choirs devoting themselves to praising the Almighty."[97]

Gardening is always in demand, for everywhere in the Summerland are beautifully arrayed flowers, trees and plants of all kinds. These plantings have been designed and implemented by souls who love this type of occupation and who enjoyed gardening while on Earth. They can stop at any time to take a break or switch to something else. They have no boss that attempts to exert control over them. They are engaged in creating and enhancing greater beauty in what is already a beautiful environment. The more they do, the greater skill they acquire. They may continue until they choose to move on to another occupation for their spiritual advancement.

Monsignor Benson speaks of those who plan and design buildings, and how anyone with interest in almost any field can get started.

In all major building operations the method followed is the same, but the methods of the spirit world have to be learnt, and the work of the architects and builders, with their various expert assistants, is among some of the most important in the spirit world. As all descriptions of employment are open to anyone who has the taste for such work, that of the architect and builder is, likewise, free to all who express a preference for continuing their earthly occupation, or who wish to turn to something new. The wish to do so is really all that is required, although, naturally, an aptitude is a great help. But it is very surprising how quickly efficiency is gained by the stimulus of desire. The "wish to do" becomes translated into the "ability to do" in a very short time. Keen interest and predilection [fondness] for the work are all that are asked.[98]

What a difference from here on Earth, where often several years' experience is required to get a job, with credit checks, aptitude tests, personality tests, drug tests, criminal record checks, etc. And, there is no need for money. What freedom!

Another type of work that souls enjoy is the making of very special fabrics. It is reported that weaving tapestries is quite an art form, and there are courses of study available to learn the craft. These courses include experimenting on how to create types of cloth, as well as the many design possibilities. The halls where fabrics are made are able to supply an extensive variety of tapestries for decoration purposes in the many varied habitations and structures.

There are countless other types of work opportunities. For example, even though doctors are no longer required due to the perfect health of souls in the afterlife, they can provide guidance to doctors on Earth. In fact, as some afterlife accounts reveal, sometimes the hands of surgeons are guided by doctors from the afterlife.

Scientists are able to move forward with what they had been researching on Earth. No matter what field of research, there are abundant possibilities for new discoveries about how things work and how to improve the quality of life, both in the afterlife, as well as on Earth.

People who are not used to working in their earth lives will have wonderful opportunities to embrace joyful tasks in the afterlife. All souls will discover that work helping others gives them joy within their spirit bodies and minds. In the afterlife, the need will be readily apparent for such activity, as entrance into the Summerland and higher realms requires active involvement in supportive and caring activities. Certain souls who are not used to work have often not reached a level of adequate purification from lower desires that would distract them or cause them to have inappropriate or inharmonious thought and action. If that is the case, they will not be ready for the Summerland. Rather, the soul will still need to work through one or more lower levels such as are available in Purgatory.

Once the soul is clear of its negative habits, he or she will be fully attuned with what remains—their true divine nature, with its natural innate longing to "work" for the sheer joy of contributing and being a part of an evolving and loving universal divine plan.

28

Cities in Eternity

Numerous descriptions of cities and urban complexes where souls dwell in the afterlife are found in the accounts of NDEs and telepathic writing. Afterlife cities are commonly described with adjectives such as beautiful and wondrous, but also as "indescribable," "crystalline, colorful, full of light," and "superior to anything that can be found on Earth." Fantastic domes, houses, and towering structures have been reported—all within grounds of splendidly landscaped gardens, huge statuesque fountains, and comfortable colored walkways.

Dannion Brinkley, in his book *Saved by the Light*, reported that during his near-death experience he visited a city of cathedrals built of crystals that glowed from an internal light. He could feel power pulsating from the city, and he knew instantly and intuitively that it was "a place of learning."

Like wingless birds, we swept into a city of cathedrals. These cathedrals were made entirely of a crystalline substance that glowed with a light that shone powerfully from within. We stood before one. I felt small and insignificant next to this architectural masterpiece. Clearly this had been built by angels to show the grandeur of God.... It had spires as high and pointed as the great cathedrals of France, and walls as massive and powerful as those of the Mormon Tabernacle in Salt Lake City. The walls were made of large glass bricks that glowed from within. These structures were not related to a specific religion of any kind. They were a monument to the glory of God.[99]

George Ritchie describes a city he saw from a distance using telescopic sight during his NDE. The city, as well as its inhabitants, radiated great light.

A glowing, seemingly endless city, bright enough to be seen over all the unimaginable distance between. The brightness seemed to shine from the very walls and streets of this place, and from beings, which I could now discern moving about within it. In fact, the city and everything in it seemed to be made of light.[100]

Reverend G. Vale Owen cites a description given by his mother in the afterlife of a city that has less light, but is beautiful nonetheless. This city is probably located at a lower plane or frequency relative to the previously described cities of light:

We sighted the city and descended before the principal gateway, by which we entered the main thoroughfare. It ran straight through the city and emerged through another gateway on the other side. On each side of this broad street there were large houses, or palaces, in spacious grounds, the residences of the principal officials of that district of which the city itself was the capital....
We saw the perfection of both buildings and horticulture. For each building had a typical garden to match it both in color and design.[101]

Monsignor Benson speaks of a beautiful city in the Summerland:

As we approached the city, it was possible for us to gather some idea of its extensive proportions. It was, I hardly need say, totally unlike anything I had yet seen. It consisted of a large number of stately buildings each of which was surrounded with magnificent gardens and trees, with here and there pools of glittering water, clear as crystal, yet reflecting every shade of colour known to Earth, with many other tints to be seen nowhere but in the realms of spirit.

It must not be imagined that these beautiful gardens bore the slightest resemblance to anything to be seen upon the Earthplane. Earthly gardens at their best and finest are of the very poorest by comparison with these that we now beheld, with their wealth of perfect colorings and their exhalations of heavenly perfumes. To walk upon the lawns with such a profusion of nature about us held us spellbound.[102]

What a difference between the delightful beauty of this afterlife city compared to the crowds and streets of cities on Earth, with their buildings crammed together, poor air quality, and the hectic rush of urban life. Benson's description continues:

I had no conception of a city of eternal beauty, as far removed from an earthly city as the light of day is from black night. Here were fine broad thoroughfares of emerald green lawns in perfect cultivation, radiating, like the spokes of a wheel, from a central building which, as we could see, was the hub of the whole city. There was a great shaft of pure light descending upon the dome of this building, and we felt instinctively...that in this temple we could together send up our thanks to the Great Source of all, and that there we should find none other than the Glory of God in Truth.

The buildings were not of any great height as we should measure and compare with earthly structures, but they were for the most part extremely broad. It is impossible to tell of what materials they were composed because they were essentially spirit fabrics. The surface of each smooth as of marble, yet it had the delicate texture and translucence of alabaster, while each building sent forth, as it were, into the adjacent air, a stream of light of the palest shade of colouring. Some of the buildings were carved with designs of foliage and flowers.... And over all was the light of heaven shining evenly and uninterruptedly, so that nowhere were there dark places.[103]

In these transcendent afterlife cities there is the complete absence of the typical commercial negotiations, trading, or business dealings that take place within Earth cities. Commercial activity as we on Earth know it is simply not necessary in the spirit world. Instead, these cities are centers for the various halls of learning. Many of these halls were erected ages ago. Each hall occupies a large area of ground and each is surrounded by beautiful gardens.

Some reports state that cities have no vehicular traffic—souls can either walk or simply teleport themselves to various locations on broad avenues of either grass or beautiful stone and crystalline pavements.

The Book of Revelation describes a vast city of gold, with colors similar to gemstones.[104] Several sources relate the various cities in the afterlife to the various levels or planes there. They point out that a soul will go to their specific level or city based on their ability to dwell therein, which naturally depends on how they have lived their life on Earth—following the natural, spiritual law of "like attracts like." Cities in the afterlife are centers of healing; of education; of science; of inspiration, of beautiful gardens, parks, and fountains; of government, to the degree it is necessary; of music, theater, and the arts; and of cosmic history.

❧ 29 ❧

Halls of Learning

Various afterlife sources, when addressing what souls do in the afterlife, not only talk about services performed, but the ongoing education of the soul. Once we make our transition, we have access to greater stores of knowledge, yet it is always up to our God-given free will how soon we commence to learn. Classes can be attended part-time or in some cases full-time and are available to all who are eager to learn and who are prepared for the experience. Often souls reach the stage of wanting to progress in their lessons and graduate to higher and higher grades, pressing on to states of greater illumination and power.

Mrs. M. T. Longley, a spiritual lecturer and medium from the early twentieth century, spoke of the afterlife's halls of learning in her book entitled *Death*:

In the great schools of spirit instruction and of experimentation, minds are trained—not crowded; they are stimulated to the expansion of their inherent qualities, wisely led to the unfoldment of the intuitive faculties that respond to the forces of the universe and absorb knowledge therefrom; are quickened in vibration to an understanding of law and of life's problems.

All the students, all the thinkers, philosophers, scientists and workers of the ages are alive; they have gone forward to wider fields of experience, but they are not so engaged in further exploitation of Life's mysteries that they give no attention to the needs and the ignorance of humanity; nay, they are busy for the race; they are inspirers, teachers, guides and helpers to multitudes who seek for understanding, for truth, and they have schools, colleges, temples of art, of literature, of science, of philosophy, of all brands of learning for the service of the eager souls who thirst for the light and knowledge that was denied them here.

Death to the progressive is an arising; it is a glorious promotion; and uplifting to a higher grade of all good; a change of base to a grander and a better world.[105]

There are many buildings devoted to the pursuit of learning the sciences as well as the arts. Reports refer to their "magnificent edifices" and the imperishable materials from which they are constructed that are more beautiful than the building materials on Earth.

Souls experience great joy when they are free to study what interests them. The improved memory of the soul whose mind is no longer encased in a brain makes learning easier. Some reports even indicate that the memory will not just be improved but work perfectly and unfailingly, removing any stress or tedious aspect to acquiring more knowledge about subjects of interest to the soul. Not only the memory, but also the ability to comprehend or understand concepts is also improved.

Many souls had strong ambitions while on Earth to study a particular field, but were unable due to having to struggle to make a living, which took all their time. It is so uplifting for a soul to finally be able to achieve knowledge about a most-loved subject, such desire having been held for a very long time.

Some reports indicate a "Montessori" approach to learning, where each student is free to pursue their studies on their own schedule. Schools are also designed for the comfort of the students and have surrounding gardens, adding beauty and greater enjoyment to the soul's experience.

What an ideal way to study! This type of learning eliminates the stress faced by today's university students on Earth. What a joy it will be to learn more about whatever interests us!

The book, *Life Between Life,* is about Dr. Joel Whitton's thirteen years of research using hypnotic regression to take his clients back to their afterlife experience prior to their current embodiment. Whitton believes that souls who are the most interested in advancing or evolving spend much of their time in the afterlife studying—they are "firmly committed to their own evolutionary progress."

Most of Dr. Whitton's subjects have found themselves hard at work in vast halls of learning equipped with libraries and seminar rooms. Doctors and lawyers, for example, have spoken of studying their respective disciplines during the interlife while others remember applying themselves to such subjects as "the laws of the universe" and other metaphysical topics. Some people even tell of studying subjects that defy description because they have no earthly counterpart.[106]

One of Whitton's subjects explained that we have to work toward becoming more Godlike, to get back to God. She states that many higher planes exist, that each one we evolve to will get us closer to that goal, and that there is no end to the learning process.

~ 30 ~

Inspirational Colleges of Music
and the Arts

The arts play a significant role in the beauty, joy and peace of the afterlife environment. Numerous halls or colleges exist for their study. These include the performing arts of music, dance and theater; the visual arts of drawing, painting, sculpting and architecture; and literature including poetry, prose and drama. We will focus on the various aspects of afterlife music in this chapter.

Reports describe numerous programs that teach composition for various types of uplifting and inspirational music. Other courses teach how to play music on any of the complete range of musical instruments—any instruments that exist on Earth, as well as others unique to the heaven world. Also, there are classes for the training of the singing voice.

Color is usually associated with descriptions of music in the afterlife. And despite the abundance of beautiful color and beautiful music, it is never too much. They both blend harmoniously into the environment and are never disconcerting or unpleasant. They present a perfect combination of sound and sight.

Some afterlife sources report that having knowledge about music helps souls to understand many aspects of spiritual life, because music plays such an important role. It is not necessary to become an expert, but with an understanding of music and harmony comes a greater degree of appreciation and enjoyment.

There are also extensive libraries containing books about music, as well as all of the compositions that are of a higher uplifting order. It is reported that many of these works have been improved upon by their composers after these composers have transitioned to the afterlife. The libraries also contain a complete history of music going all the way back to their very origins, enabling interested souls to follow the course of musical developments over time. It is noteworthy that many popular songs on Earth are *not* heard or included in the libraries, as they have a harmful effect on the emotions and soul.

In fact, the musically inclined and, eventually, all souls entering the afterlife, come to understand that different varieties of earth-based music have no place in the heaven world, except perhaps in historical archives, also referred to as the Akashic Records. Souls who may have enjoyed certain types of music that are actually not harmonic and do not qualify as useful in the afterlife are occasionally, if briefly, disappointed by their absence. In literally all cases, this disappointment is short-lived, for this "music of the spheres," as the ancients called the most beautiful pieces set down by the master composers, are unbelievably scintillating and transcendent musical compositions and performances that utterly eclipse so much of what passed for music in the earthly realms.

Some sources report that there are places where musical instruments are manufactured. The question remains how much of that has any semblance to earthlike manufacturing techniques versus the more spiritual ways of focusing thought power to re-form energy and matter. The answer may depend on which plane this occurs as well as a particular soul's abilities and comprehension.

There are also courses for studying music at Heaven's exalted level, and then acting to transmit these higher musical ideas to composers on Earth. There are always a number of souls who are literal angelic muses, who are busy giving the gift of heavenly music by inspiring receptive individual artists on Earth.

Concerts are a regular occurrence, and are greatly enjoyed because the music is not only exceedingly beautiful but creates a holistic experience that includes wonderful thought-forms. Benson gives a detailed description of a concert given by some two hundred musicians, with its many wonderful effects. He reports that the instruments sounded like those on Earth but their tone quality sounded purer and perfectly blended. Here is his lengthy description of the beautiful light show the concert created:

The opening movement was of a subdued nature as regards its volume of sound, and we noticed that the instant the music commenced a bright light seemed to rise up from the direction of the orchestra until it floated, in a flat surface, level with the topmost seats, where it remained as an iridescent cover to the whole amphitheatre. As the music proceeded, this broad sheet of light grew in strength and density, forming, as it were, a firm foundation for what was to follow....
Presently, at equal spaces round the circumference of the theatre, four towers of light shot up into the sky in long tapering pinnacles of luminosity. They remained poised for a moment, and then slowly descended, becoming broader in girth as they did so, until they assumed the outward appearance of four circular towers, each surmounted with a dome, perfectly proportioned. In the meanwhile, the central area of light had thickened still more, and was beginning to rise slowly in the shape of an immense dome covering the whole theatre. This continued to ascend steadily

until it seemed to reach a very much greater height than the four towers, while the most delicate colours were diffused throughout the whole of the etheric structure....

The musical sounds sent up by the orchestra were creating, up above their heads, this immense musical thought-form, and the shape and perfection of this form rested entirely upon the purity of the musical sounds, the purity of the harmonies, and a freedom from any pronounced dissonance. The form of the music must be pure to produce a pure form.

It must not be assumed that every description of discord was absent. To lack discord would be to produce monotony, but the discords were legitimately used and properly resolved.

By now the great musical thought-form had assumed what appeared to be its limit of height, and it remained stationary and steady. The music was still being played, and in response to it the whole colouring of the dome changed, first to one shade, then to another, and many times to a delicate blend of a number of shades according to the variation in theme or movement of the music.[107]

This, of course, was a sound and light show better than anything possible on Earth. It is one more thing to look forward to when the time arrives for entering the afterlife.

Beautiful concerts affect their environments, as well as their audience. A description of the effects of music has come to us through Reverend G. Vale Owen:

[The heavenly music] made everything more lovely, not only beautiful, but lovely, too—for there is a difference in meaning of these two words as I use them here. All our faces took on a more lovely hue and expression, the trees became deeper in color, and the atmosphere gradually grew into a vapor of tints like a rainbow. But the vapor did not obscure anything; it seemed to bring everything nearer together rather. The water reflected the rainbow tints, and our clothing also became intensified in color. Moreover, the animals and birds about us also responded.

One white bird I remember especially. Her beautiful milky feathers gradually grew brighter and, when I saw her last, before she flew into a grove, she shone like gold burnished and glowing, like transparent light or fire. Then, as the mists slowly faded away, we all became, and everything became, normal once again. But the effect remained, and if I could give it a name, I should say it was "peace."

...For music enters into so many phases of our life here, and, indeed, all seems music in these spheres of light—music and blended color and beauty, all breathing love among all.[108]

Betty Eadie describes a simple but extremely powerful melody she experienced during her near-death experience. She felt that the music conveyed powerful healing and loving energy, unlike much of the music we hear on Earth.

It was a tone, similar to a note of music, but was universal and seemed to fill all the space around me. It was followed by another tone at a different pitch, and soon I noticed something of a melody—a vast, cosmic song that soothed and comforted me. The tones produced soft vibrations, and as they touched me I knew that they possessed the power to heal. I knew that anything touched by these tones would receive the effects of their healing; they were like spiritual salve, expressions of love that mended broken spirits.

I learned from the escorts traveling with me that not all musical tones are healing—that some can create within us negative emotional responses. I understood now that while I was on Earth, Satan had used these negative tones in music, which actually produced illness in my mind and body.[109]

In the Summerland and higher levels, harmony is a fundamental law. Conflicts do not occur there, which ensures a most harmonious environment, along with the much greater roles that beautiful music and color play. Musicians and other artists are free to focus on their creativity, without human-based motives of fame, reputation, or power. Music is considered essential, as it adds so much to the beauty of the environment. In fact, souls report that now that they have been in the heaven world, it would simply be impossible to imagine it without its pervading divine natural sounds, intonations, and harmonious music.

It is reported that when a soul leaves the Earth and comes to the afterlife, their entire attitude about music changes. On Earth music is viewed by most as an enjoyable diversion...an option, but not a necessity. In the Summerland it is a part of life. It exists as a part of the natural environment, even when it is not played by the souls that live there. It provides great joy with its accompanying color, and is part of an incredibly beautiful environment provided by our loving Father that is far removed from the imagined "emptiness" that some mistakenly believe will characterize the afterlife.

❧ 31 ❧

Fascinating Halls of Science

As with many advanced human endeavors, help "from on high" is often, by the grace of our Creator, made available to souls on Earth. For example, when scientists on Earth make breakthrough discoveries, they have frequently been assisted by higher, "science-oriented" souls in the afterlife. Quite often the Earth scientists are not at all aware of the help and guidance they have received. The laboratories in the spirit world are of course significantly more advanced than those on Earth. However, as afterlife communications confirm, numerous discoveries are being held back, because there are some on Earth who are not sufficiently evolved to use them solely for good.

Scientists that are recently transitioned from Earth are able to work alongside longer-term residents of the heaven world to continue their research. There they enjoy greater freedom enabling them to advance the work they had begun on Earth. All the various scientific, as well as engineering subjects, are examined utilizing the vast resources available in the hereafter. It has been reported that all major scientific discoveries have been the result of Earth scientists being inspired by afterlife scientists!

In the afterlife, inventions are often developed that are not needed there. They are developed for the benefit of those on Earth. For example, because the laws applicable in the afterlife are different from the Earth, there is no need for certain inventions that enable souls to travel faster, because travel in the afterlife is as fast as thought. Furthermore, there is no need for inventions to save lives, because souls are imperishable. Many other inventions that make life easier, more enjoyable, and safer on Earth are of no specific use in the hereafter.

There is a certain degree of sadness among afterlife scientists, because many of their inventions must be held back from the Earth. The greed and selfishness of certain Earth scientists and businessmen have been the cause of this problem. It was never intended that scientific discoveries sent from the afterlife be misused, resulting in suffering, chaos and/or widespread destruction of life. Earth-based scientists who have engaged in this sort of wrongdoing have a great karmic debt to pay for the illicit fame and materialistic self-centeredness they chose to experience while on Earth.

When mankind finally reaches the stage of using its free will in the direction of the common good, there will be a great influx of wonderful, and largely undreamed-of developments inspired by afterlife scientists. But this progress will only occur when it goes hand in hand with humanity's widespread spiritual progress. On that bright, sunlit day, the Earth and the afterlife world will enjoy much clearer communication, and life on Earth, as spiritual teachers, Biblical prophets, and ancient sages have long predicted, will begin to resemble life in the heaven world. People will then know the consequences for the misuse of power throughout human history as they simultaneously rejoice in the dawning of a wonderful new era for mankind and all life on Earth.

Scientific research in the afterlife yields great joy for the researcher, as grand new spiritual laws governing the functioning of the universe are revealed. Once the transition occurs, there will unfold not just a whole new world but entire dimensions throughout the universe! Scientists will then discover and begin to utilize unlimited and undreamed-of resources in studying the mysteries of the cosmos.

From testimonies of the afterlife, we learn that apart from any halls of research and invention, "scientists of the spirit" are active in creating vast new worlds, lending support to the theologians and philosophers who have, since ancient times, speculated that God's creation is infinite, going on both spatially and in terms of time, forever. According to the accounts from advanced souls received by Reverend Owen, the entire operation and the continual expansion of the universe is made possible by high souls of wisdom applying scientific laws on a cosmic scale barely imaginable to us. They keep things running smoothly by their ongoing adjustments.

We, acting always in perfect obedience to laws laid down by those higher and wiser than ourselves, concentrate our wills on the movement of certain vibrations which become deflected and transmuted into other qualities of vibration, and thus change is wrought....

It is by this method that we deal with the actions of men, and the course of nature in all its parts. There are manifold classes and companies who have in charge [who are in charge of] the various departments of creation—mineral, vegetable, animal, human, terrestrial, solar, and stellar. Beyond this... the stars are grouped together and dealt with by hierarchies qualified for that great task.

It is by this same method, then, of the transmutation of energy that systems are gradually developed into worlds, and these worlds furnished with form, and then enabled to produce vegetation and animal life. But, this being so, you will note that all life, and all development, is consequent on the operation of spiritual energy obeying the dictates of the will of spiritual beings. This once grasped, blind force disappears, and intention takes its place—intention of intelligent and powerful spiritual workers of various grades operating according to certain fixed laws but, within the bounds of laws free and mighty.[110]

We begin to realize that our loving Creator has established a grand hierarchy of unnumbered evolutions of souls who progressively master and joyfully implement the universal laws of creation. It is inspiring to understand how everything (for example, the Earth's orbit around the Sun, and the Moon's around the Earth) is kept in balance, not by "blind force," but by loving and highly developed souls under God's direction.

❦ 32 ❦

Government in Divine Order

The afterlife has little need for government as the concept is applied on Earth. It is reported that if there *does* happen to be any form of misconduct or disobedience, the wiser spirits who have earned a mantle of authority in this respect have the guilty party take a course of instruction. After that, if disobedience continues, the soul is relocated to a lower plane or dimension, to further learn what they need to know to advance higher. This is reportedly a rare occurrence, except in the lowest realms. In the higher realms, souls are more eager to learn, and are placed progressively at levels that are devoid of any sense of conflict or dissent.

Some reports indicate that those souls who rule over the various afterlife realms have been there for thousands of years, and are from higher realms than where they rule. They have tremendous experience in dealing with souls. Their characteristics include great kindness and patience, as well as empathy and understanding of humanity. In addition, they need to have a tremendous amount of knowledge, which is made possible by the enhanced memories that souls from higher realms enjoy. That knowledge includes their awareness of much information about the souls under their supervision. The sum total of these attributes amounts to every leader having great wisdom, enabling them to provide appropriate leadership and guidance as required.

Politics and politicians as these are known on Earth are completely unnecessary and, one could say, blissfully absent from the afterlife. In fact, rulers in afterlife governments actually preside rather than rule, being aided by clearly evident natural law, which provides powerful and often-immediate feedback for souls to work within specified, as well as intuitively understood guidelines. In other words, souls who may begin to think about disobeying one of these natural laws, usually realize, due to the clearly apparent negative consequences, that they don't want to act wrongly! Thus, the need for individual souls to be "governed" by others is significantly less than on Earth. Monsignor Benson describes this "self-governing" process:

> Our "government" is by natural laws, and therefore the best in the whole universe. Better, a million times, than anything that could ever be devised from man's ingenuity. Natural laws need no enforcing; they enforce themselves.
>
> The natural laws on Earth are not so easily perceived. Few, for instance, can see the natural law at work when thoughts are emitted. We can here, and their effect. Obviously, some of those laws have no effect whatever on Earth. If you had tried to shift your physical body by the power of thought, as you are able to do [here]..., you would have remained where you were. Still, the natural laws are not the only means of what might be called government here....
>
> Each realm has its ruler. That's not a strictly accurate term, though we do use it....
>
> He presides, and that is very different. I'm talking about the realms of light now. You can see for yourself how much pleasanter and easier it makes life. No falling of one government merely to make way for another equally bad or stupid or ineffective. No political fanatics with insane and inane ideas, and what is most important, no individuals holding office who are totally unfitted for it.[111]

Emanuel Swedenborg points out that in the highest realms there is no government in any sense, because a pure and mutual love prevails over all! In the realms below that, which Swedenborg terms "the Lord's spiritual kingdom," governments of different types exist, depending on the needs of different soul groups. (Remember that Swedenborg uses language over two hundred years old.)

They have governors, few or more, according to the need of the society in which they are. They also have laws, according to which they live together. The governors administer all things according to the laws. They understand them because they are wise; and in doubtful cases they are enlightened by the Lord....

All the forms of government agree in this, that they regard the general good as their end, and in that, the good of every individual....

The Lord, who loves all, and from divine love ordains that the common good shall be the source of good to every individual, and that every individual shall receive good in proportion as he loves the common good....

They [the governors] are in love and wisdom more than others, and...they will well to all from love, and from wisdom know how to provide that the good they desire may be realized. They who are of this character, do not domineer and command imperiously, but minister and serve....

Nor do they account themselves greater than others, but less; for they esteem the good of society and of their neighbor in the first place, but their own in the last....

Nevertheless they enjoy honor and glory. They dwell in the midst of that society, in a more elevated situation than others, and inhabit magnificent palaces. They also accept glory and honor, not for the sake of themselves, but for the sake of obedience; for all in heaven know that honor and glory are from the Lord, and that for this reason they ought to be obeyed.[112]

We are thus reminded of the words that Jesus gave to his disciples:

And whosoever will be chief among you, let him be your servant.[113]

Betty Eadie confirms that love is behind these "servant rulers," as it is behind all life activity in the higher worlds. She also mentions that self-love of the divine within ourselves is required for our love of others, because only then can we identify that same divinity in others.

With all of this understanding, I understood again that love is supreme. Love must govern. Love always governs the spirit, and the spirit must be strengthened to rule the mind and flesh. I understood the natural order of love everywhere. First, we must love the Creator. This is the greatest love we can have (although we may not know this until we meet Him). Then we must love ourselves. I knew that without feelings of self-love that the love we feel for others is counterfeit. Then, we must love all others as ourselves. As we see the light of Christ in ourselves, we will see it in others too, and it will become impossible not to love that part of God in them.[114]

Eadie helps us grasp that, yes, there is great emphasis within the heart of all spiritual teachings on the importance of being "selfless," of aligning with our true nature, of acting with compassion and charity towards our fellow humans, of approaching our life in the standard of "selfless service." And, at the same time, we must not harbor any negative attitudes or feelings about ourselves. In this human condition, this is accomplished when we awaken to the soul's true mission, namely to identify with the part of us which is God, known variously in religious traditions as the Higher Self, the Christ Self, the I AM Presence, the Divine Self, the Atman, etc. For it is only from a center of love for our own unique yet, at the same time, one-with-God self that we can radiate true love, the love that is our divine birthright, to other souls.

❧ 33 ❧

Religion and Worship
in the Afterlife

According to several afterlife sources, souls are free to continue the type of worship they were accustomed to on Earth. Churches of various denominations are available. In the Summerland, those with great faith in their particular religion continue practicing their beliefs. In the book, *Death and the Afterlife* by Andrew Jackson Davis, the author states:

> *Jews still believe in the doctrine of their fathers—Abraham, Isaac, and Jacob; the Roman Catholics hold the same views they did before death; and there are other sects... who think and believe in the same thing and forms of faith they learned on Earth.*[115]

This continuity of belief is largely due to the soul's need to remain with what is familiar, until such time as the soul evolves through the course of their experience to the place where it is easy to embrace a more unified understanding of the spirit that is shared by more evolved souls. The religion learned on Earth helps souls feel "at home," but eventually all souls perceive how the true aspects of their former beliefs integrate with their spiritual life and our Creator. Sooner or later souls move beyond the limitations found within their particular church creeds and join those who simply worship God in gratitude for His gift of eternal and beautiful life.

On the higher planes there is a unity of praise and gratitude for God that is not segregated. This communal expression of love and worship of the Creator contains no dogmas, ideologies or creeds. No one is expected to believe blindly, as their free will determines their level of faith every step of the way. Each soul progresses in the afterlife at their own unique pace. But it can be predicted that, in the higher realms of Heaven, all souls enjoy a degree of divine love and spiritual enlightenment, which renders separate religions and religious doctrines altogether unnecessary. Whereas on Earth, they so often served to advance the soul's spiritual progress, at a certain level of the heaven world, individual religions will be unknown, except as historical artifact. This is not written presumptuously or with any hint of denigration toward any religion. It is simply the ultimate realization that the Creator and His infinite creation cannot possibly be encompassed by a single earthly religion, nor for that matter, all of them combined. Souls in the higher realms can clearly see for themselves the glorious and beautiful life provided.

There are many things that may not be fully understood at these levels, but not understanding everything is acceptable. Souls are asked to just accept, as they are, any wonders of the universe that are too difficult at a particular time to understand. A soul can still progress from one step to the next without all-knowledge.

It is probably much easier in the Summerland than here on Earth to rely on faith in the goodness of all things without a full understanding of them. For in the Summerland, goodness and love are seen and felt all around. Compare that to the difficulty of having such a strong faith on Earth, where we're surrounded by so much sorrow, poverty, confusion, and imperfection.

Monsignor Benson shares some rather blunt observations pertaining to people who have been heavily indoctrinated and, in many cases not taught any higher spiritual truths. He reports that they can be particularly obstinate in clinging to their limited and erroneous beliefs, holding fast to ideas that don't fit in with the realities of the afterlife:

> *[They] may be good folk, but are completely dominated by orthodox religious views, and this type, if anything, is perhaps among the worst of them all to deal with!*
>
> *There is, over and above these, a certain type of religious mind that causes us a great deal of trouble, and it is associated with those people upon Earth whose religion is of a very crude, elementary description, ...[based] upon a literal interpretation of the scriptures according to their own primitive ideas....*
>
> *They picture themselves spending all eternity in some form of simple worship, which incorporates a vast deal of hymn singing and conversational quotation from the scriptural books.*
>
> *You can imagine for yourself something of the shock that awaits such souls when they arrive here in the spirit world, to find that they are totally mistaken in the true state of things. At first they will gravitate to others of their own kind, if we find it impossible, for the moment, to convince them of their errors. At length, their home-made 'heaven' will begin to bore them, until they become thoroughly dissatisfied with their life and surroundings. Then we can step in and introduce them to a normal, natural way of living in the spirit world.*[116]

Emanuel Swedenborg reports that there are "doctrines and sermons" in the afterlife which are basically in agreement. What is important is a soul's internal experience with the divine while living a loving life.

> *Real divine worship in the heavens does not consist in frequenting temples and listening to sermons, but in a life of love, charity, and faith, according to doctrine. Sermons in the temples serve only as means of instruction in the conduct of life....*
>
> *It is believed in the world that divine worship consists merely in going to church, hearing sermons, attending the sacrament of the holy supper three or four times a year, and in other forms of worship prescribed by the church; to which may be*

added, the setting apart of particular time for prayer, and a devout manner while engaged in it.... These are externals which ought to be observed, but they are of no avail unless there be an internal from which they proceed.[117]

In other words, people just going through the motions without an internally strong focus and attunement with God's loving light would be missing the entire point of their actions. More evolved souls likely have deeper inner spiritual experiences and a greater understanding of true religion and spirituality. Their experiences would feel much more real and attuned with divine light.

Swedenborg also addresses the false belief among certain Christians that non-Christians will be missing out on their divine heritage:

It is a common opinion that those who are born out of the church, who are called Heathen or Gentiles, cannot be saved, because they have not the Word, and thus are ignorant of the Lord, without whom there can be no salvation. Nevertheless it may be known that they also are saved.... The mercy of the Lord is universal, that is, extended toward every individual....

Every person who thinks from any enlightened reason, may see that no man is born for hell; for the Lord is love itself, and it is agreeable to His love that all be saved....

That Gentiles are saved as well as Christians, may be known to those who understand what it is that makes heaven with man; for heaven is in man, and those who have heaven in themselves enter heaven after death. It is heaven in man to acknowledge a Divine, and to be led by Him. The first and primary thing of every religion is to acknowledge a Divine.[118]

Based on his numerous travels and experiences in the afterlife, Swedenborg acknowledges that our Creator's mercy and love for His children is supreme, that God's love would not exclude anyone. What is most essential for souls is *an acknowledgement of God within themselves individually*. This acknowledgement can then evolve to the greater joy of *knowing and feeling* God within.

Reverend G. Vale Owen reports that Arnel, a highly evolved soul in the afterlife, describes men as having unnecessarily limited themselves and their attunement with God through over-dependence on the Bible. Progressive revelation, whereby not only Jesus, but also the great Hebrew prophets and various saints and holy men and women throughout history who have continued to illumine mankind, should not be ignored. As Jesus advised us, it is best to "Believe not every spirit, but try the spirits whether they are of God."[119] We must utilize our power of discrimination to distinguish what is true from all the rest. Love for Jesus Christ shines through all Owen's communications:

So you will understand, my son, that the mistake men made was to hamper a living, moving Life with a Book. They regarded that Book not as what it was and is, wonderful, beautiful and mostly true, but as both infallible and also complete. But the Life of Christ has been continued in the world and is continued today....

Men are beginning to see this now and to understand that if He spoke by His angels to good men of old, so does He speak to them today. These men go forward, glad of the beacon-light behind [the Bible], but with greater gladness toward the more radiant light ahead.... He goes before you. Follow Him without fear. He promised He would lead you. Follow Him.[120]

Our love and an intense desire for the truth are prerequisites to finding it. Our humble prayers and supplications for divine guidance bring us grace and allow such help to be given to us. But due to the law of free will, heavenly emissaries cannot help unless we first ask.

Betty Eadie, based on her near-death experience, addresses why we don't have a single religion. The logic is clear that souls both on Earth, as well as in the afterlife, need "stepping stones" that provide familiarity until they're ready for their next level.

> *Why didn't God give us only one church, one pure religion? The answer came to me with the purest of understanding. Each of us, I was told, is at a different level of spiritual development and understanding. Each person is therefore prepared for a different level of spiritual knowledge. All religions upon the Earth are necessary because there are people who need what they teach. People in one religion may not have a complete understanding of the Lord's gospel and never will have while in the religion. But that religion is used as a steppingstone to further knowledge. Each church fulfills spiritual needs that perhaps others cannot fill.[121]*

In the more advanced planes, where souls are no longer practicing their separate religions, they instead focus on increasing their attunement and oneness with the abundance of light and love prevalent in those spheres. Souls feel a strong attunement with the life source and eagerly embrace opportunities to experience an increase in their light. Sister Frances Banks refers to a "Ceremony of Light" she attended:

> *This formation of thought, this deep concerted concentration, springs from the deep desire to experience Life and yet more Life, to unite with the Supreme Essence, to realize as far as one's present consciousness will allow that Life is expansion, that Light is but the widening of one's inner perceptions.[122]*

These ceremonies of light contribute to a soul's ability to overcome blockages in their personality. Barriers caused by negative feelings and memories in the conscious and sub-conscious mind need to be properly understood to allow healing light to enter in—for attuning with and rising into the higher realms.

❧ 34 ❧

Telepathic Communication
From and Within the Afterlife

Telepathic communication is viewed as an amazing phenomenon for us very earthbound humans, because it enables us to communicate with others, not only at a potentially great distance across the Earth, but also with dimensions far removed from our everyday reality. Telepathy between "earthlings," as well as telepathy between a soul on Earth and a soul "on the other side," such as in the form of telepathic or automatic writing, is currently not widely recognized on Earth. This broad lack of recognition of genuine telepathic communication, not to mention the outright skepticism of many, is in recent decades strongly countermanded by a number of credible scientific studies.

The subject of telepathy, while now common in Hollywood movies and on some of the more daring cable channels, continues to be largely missing from mainstream media programming. In contrast to our temporary sojourns on Earth, telepathy is easily the main, indeed, the essential form of communication in the afterlife.

Since souls can move themselves about using just the power of thought, it makes sense that thoughts can be communicated from one soul to another. Thoughts are more powerful and surely more tangible than many on Earth believe.

Receiving a telepathic message is reported by one source to sound like the sender is speaking close to the ear. Of course, there is little or no "sound" generated as we would experience the same message conveyed between two persons on Earth.

There appears to be no limit to the distance a thought can be transmitted. In the spirit world, sending a definite message to another soul or even thinking affectionately about that soul results in those thoughts being received. This ability is simply accepted without a full understanding of the mechanics of how it works.

Several spiritual teachings acknowledge the reality of "thought-forms." Monsignor Benson discusses these thought-forms, and that thought for those on Earth is not just dependent on the physical brain:

The incarnate do not realize the force and power of thought.... Every thought that passes with force and purpose through the mind of an Earth dweller is projected from his mind as a thought-form. To speak unscientifically, it is registered, at least for a time, upon the surrounding ether. It depends, of course, upon the thought itself, and of what it consists.... If the thought is directed towards some friend who is now resident in the spirit world, that thought, if it is properly directed with purpose and intent, will inevitably reach that friend. It will reach him or her just as it is sent, no more or less good, bad or indifferent.

Thought may be invisible to the majority of Earth dwellers but it is very much visible to spirit folk....

Thought is upon a different plane, a higher plane of existence from that organ of the earthly body, the brain, through which thought functions on Earth. Thought is upon the same plane of existence as the mind, and the mind belongs truly to the spirit world....

In the spirit world thought has direct and instantaneous action upon whatsoever it is directed.... It is not until you come into the spirit world that you really know just what thought can do. And I do assure you, my good friend, that some of us are positively horrified when we find out for the first time![123]

This topic of the power of thought and the reality of thought-forms is fascinating. Numerous books exist on the subject including several by Annie Besant of the Theosophical Society. Others include how to work with thought-forms to achieve one's goals. Basically, this time-honored concept holds that if we establish new habit-patterns of thought, we can attract the object of these patterns.

While we are embodied on Earth, the density around our bodies and our brains makes it difficult for most of us to clearly receive the thoughts from loved ones in the spirit world. But it is truly comforting to think that our loved ones there are much more able to receive the loving thoughts we send to them.

Despite this ease of thought transference in the after-life, it is still possible to keep thoughts private. Otherwise, communication would be too stressful! Care must be taken, however, if a soul should be thinking idly, without fully recognizing what is being thought. It is essential that thoughts be kept under control, that a soul maintain awareness of what he or she is thinking so that unintended messages are not delivered.

Once a soul enters the afterlife, learning how to think properly is not difficult, although to us it may sound so! Souls simply need to be aware when they are thinking about other souls to not think in a negative or judgmental manner. In addition, if a regrettable thought about another soul occurs, it will not reach them unless the thought has sufficient energy. If it is merely an idle passing thought without such energy, no harm will be done. The knowledge that another soul could receive a negative thought if it had sufficient power or concentration behind it is enough to help souls quickly acquire the habit of thinking only positive thoughts about their brothers and sisters.

Betty Eadie, during her near-death experience, received a wonderful feeling of peace, deep love and the message that everything for her would be all right—all through a form of telepathy that included feelings and intent.

These feelings and other thoughts were communicated from spirit to spirit—from intelligence to intelligence. At first, I thought that they were using their mouths, but this was because I was used to people "speaking." They communicated much more rapidly and completely, in a manner they referred to as "pure knowledge." The closest word in English we would have to define it is telepathy, but even that doesn't describe the full process. I felt their emotions and intents. I felt their love. I experienced their feelings. And this filled me with joy because they loved me so much.... I realized that my former ability to express feelings had been almost nonexistent compared with the ability of the spirit to communicate in this pure way.[124]

How wonderful to be able to let someone else know you love them just by thinking about them and instantly sending them a loving message that they can feel! While two earth-bound souls may indeed achieve this between one another (studies confirm this does occur between certain individuals) it is unusual on Earth. But not in the afterlife.

On Earth, people can and often do "mask" their true self and appear quite different from who they really are. Such masking is extremely difficult and consequently, extremely rare in the afterlife. Thoughts can be kept private, but the basic character and intent of a soul is still clearly evident.

Imagine how life-changing it will be once we, here on Earth, develop our telepathic abilities—wearing a "mask" will no longer be possible, much less desired. The light of truth will unmask any who would practice dishonesty and corruption. Elections will produce good and honest leaders. Truth will be held in the highest regard. As a result, people will be more aware of our unity, our oneness. Polarizations of opinions will be difficult, as the "spin-factor" will be more difficult to maintain by those with various vested interests. The easy detection of lies would certainly help all people to "get on the same page" through realizing how close we are to each other and to our loving and merciful Creator. Peace on Earth and good-will to mankind would then be far, far easier to achieve!

ᴄᴡᵹ 35 ᵹꜱᴄ

Mind Power in the Afterlife

Modern psychologists, ancient philosophers and most religions teach us that a major key to happiness is the proper utilization of our "mind power." In the afterlife, our telepathically transmitted thoughts are more distinctive and far more powerful than the normal human thoughts we were accustomed to on Earth. Whether a thought is positive or negative in the afterlife, it creates an action that can quickly return to the sender. Sister Frances Banks touches on how powerful our thoughts are:

> In this new life, the potency of thought is stepped up into a frequency which permits no sidestepping. The effects are immediate. Here the thought-pattern is determinate of one's welfare, one's progress, one's happiness and joy. As one thinks, so one is...in environment, appearance and in company!
>
> We have to learn to live in this new frequency; to guard the doors of one's mind; to anticipate the boomerang action of negative emotions.[125]

In the previous chapter, it was noted that some thoughts are just "passing thoughts" without much power. Even though afterlife reporters proclaim the potency of thought power, there is a definite gradation of the power of thoughts—those with the most intensity and focus would have the most immediate effect.

After we leave the Earth, our thoughts largely determine our happiness and the progress we make. As Banks and numerous others confirm, it is important to guard our thinking due to the boomerang effect. For this reason, and considering how challenging it can be to develop the habit of right-thinking, it is wise to begin practicing while we are yet in physical embodiment.

What sounds like potential chaos regarding the power of thought, and especially negative thought in the afterlife, is mitigated by a soul's greater awareness of the categories of their thoughts. In the afterlife, the soul does have a greater ability to organize thoughts. For example, souls can be quite selective in what they "receive." It is reported that souls have an enhanced ability to mentally isolate themselves to a greater extent than on Earth. Doing this requires less concentration and conscious effort than when on Earth. It is simply due to the soul having greater natural ability because it is no longer clouded by a sluggish physical brain. Alternately, souls can much more easily open their minds to treat their senses to the wonderful colors, scents and music of the flowers, trees and plants, the waters and so many other sensations in their afterlife existence. It is far easier to be selective regarding both what one shuts out, as well as what one invites in.

The heaven world is based upon law and order that is neither oppressive or bothersome. It is simply logical and is designed to maximize beauty and peace and minimize anything that might tend to be in any way chaotic or disordered.

The significantly improved memory available to souls in the afterlife can be used to retrieve at will any appropriate information that has been stored. The excellent memory of both our conscious and subconscious minds enables us to learn and retain new facts and skills far more efficiently.

Monsignor Benson describes some of the benefits of perfect memory functioning in the afterlife:

When we are in the spirit world our memories are persistently retentive. When we follow a course of study in any subject whatsoever, we shall find that we learn easily and quickly because we are freed from the limitations that the physical body imposes upon the mind. If we are acquiring knowledge we shall retain that knowledge without fail. If we are following some pursuit where dexterity of the hands is required, we shall find that our spirit bodies respond to the impulses of our minds immediately and exactly. To learn to paint a picture, or to play upon a musical instrument, to mention two familiar mundane activities, are tasks that can be performed in a fraction of the time that they would take when we are incarnate....

Our intelligence can be increased; that is part of our progression, for progression is not only of a spiritual nature. Our minds have unlimited resources for intellectual expansion and improvement, however backward we may be when we come into the spirit world. And our intellectual progression will advance surely and steadily, according to our wish for it to do so, under the learned and able masters of all branches of knowledge and learning. And throughout our studies we shall be assisted by our unfailingly retentive memories. There will be no forgetting.[126]

Some afterlife sources state that there is a merging of the conscious and subconscious mind. Whether this is true or not, either way we will have significantly improved control of our thoughts and intentions, such that we will undoubtedly enjoy a major increase in our understanding and ability to acquire knowledge.

It is interesting to note how many people on Earth think of the afterlife as nebulous and less real than Earth life. When people hear that it is a world of thought, some conclude that its inhabitants are living in a shadow realm, one without real substance. These beliefs about the afterlife are connected to the fact that on Earth thought is usually unseen and unheard by others. Most of us believe that here on Earth our thoughts are completely private and that we can, with abandon, think what we like. (It is also falsely believed that thoughts can never harm anyone.) When people hear that the afterlife is a world of thought, they then also wrongly conclude that the entire afterlife is just as insubstantial as their own earthly thoughts. One can begin to appreciate why many individual souls really do need a significant period of orientation and adjustment upon their entry into the afterlife.

We can choose, by the grace of God, to give ourselves a joyous life. Betty Eadie describes for us the transcendent importance of the soul's thought power:

Because I knew that all creation begins with thoughts, I also knew that the creation of sin, and of guilt, and of despair, and of hope, and of love all start within us. All healing comes from within... We can create our own spiral of despair, or we can create a trampoline of happiness and attainment.[127]

In conclusion, it is most helpful in our personal evolution to practice meditation, contemplation, and prayer on a regular basis, so that our souls can experience attunement with the divine realities, with our future in the Summerland and beyond. It is by our moment-to-moment thoughts—by establishing thought patterns of loving and righteous living that inspire us, that we create our eternal future. In many ways, it can be said that we live in a mental world. In the final analysis, blessed with a mind "like the mind of God," the gift of divine grace and our own free will, we create what we will experience and ultimately, exactly who we will become.

ᨠᨠ 36 ᨠᨠ

Yes, There Is Joy and Recreation in the Afterlife!

Is there joyousness in the afterlife? Definitely! When on so many occasions the soul is filled with joy at the love and the beauty there, it is most natural to accompany that joy with sheer exclamations of pleasure, which can often take the form of laughter and delight. Laughter is of course enjoyable, and it fits perfectly into the grand design of our evolution.

After all, our Creator is the creator of all that is good. Why would such emotions as joy and good humor be lacking in Summerland? We, as sons and daughters of God, have the ability and desire to express our joy in many ways. From the Bible we find:

Blessed are ye that hunger now: for ye shall be filled. Blessed are ye that weep now: for ye shall laugh.[128]

It is reported that there are similar pleasantries enjoyed between souls in the Summerland as are enjoyed on Earth among friends. Mild jokes are still enjoyed—not using humor that would hurt another's feelings, but enjoyable observations and light-hearted banter. And, as might be supposed, it is easier to engage in this when no longer burdened by the environment of serious and tragic circumstances that exist here on Earth.

Reverend Owen recounts an example given by his mother in the afterlife of souls enjoying themselves while "practicing creation," which they sometimes gather together to do. The group concentrates their wills to manifest one particular thing, and as it appears, they can see how realistic it is. In focusing on the creation of an orange tree, the following was reported:

> *The chief points of failure were that some of the fruit was ripe and some unripe. And the leaves were not correct in color, nor the branches rightly proportioned. And so we tried one thing after another, and found ourselves a little more successful each time. You can imagine somewhat of the joy of such schooling as this, and the laughter and happy humor which result from our mistakes.*
>
> *Those among you who think that in this life we never make jokes, and never even laugh, will have to revise their ideas someday.... They will soon learn what the love of this land is, where we can be perfectly natural and unrestrained, and indeed are compelled to be so if we wish to be accepted into respectable company, as you would phrase it.... Those who live in this life— and not merely exist, or worse—learn very quickly. And the more we learn, the more we marvel at the forces at our command.[129]*

Recreation for souls can come in several forms. One is simply to make a change in one's "work," or to take up another pursuit in addition to one's work. In the afterlife, souls don't usually have to deal with fatigue of body or mind, but according to numerous testimonials, a soul enjoys occasional changes.

Learning is considered a form of recreation in the afterlife. Forms of intellectual recreation can be engaged in the halls of learning. Learning there, however, much like on Earth, can involve much more than simply spending time in a library, museum or an art exhibit. There are the studies of various disciplines leading to the creation of one's own art and music.

There is travel and exploration, which in the hereafter can be undertaken in myriad different forms.

Several persons who have experienced NDEs have described being taken on "learning tours." These tours have included studying the Akashic Records (a compendium of all human events, thoughts, words, emotions and intent ever to have occurred—reportedly stored on the etheric plane) and have often revealed insights into historical events that do not always conform to the predominant or "official" view of these events. In addition to accounts from NDEs, we know that some souls have reported via telepathic writing that they have sessions studying these records. For us on Earth it is quite amazing to contemplate studying such records, for they would not merely be a historian's dream occupation but a wondrously engaging means for any soul to witness and contemplate the full meaning of past events.

Reports include descriptions of theatrical productions about history on Earth. These are presented so as to show not only the Earth's original version of the play but also the absolute truth about the story. Sometimes even the original historical personages are available to play their own part! And sometimes previously unknown heroes and villains are revealed.

Some plays are reported to be shown that present social questions on the Earth. These plays always include a practical solution to the problem. Comedies are enjoyed and include some subjects that are considered serious on Earth, but when seen from the afterlife perspective, are laughable.

Often these plays and akashic viewing sessions take place in beautiful theatres located in equally natural settings, where architects have used great care in their design. Skilled artists from the "Hall of Fabrics" have decorated the interiors of the theaters, and skilled landscapers have focused their efforts on making the grounds especially lovely.

Some souls enjoy participating in contests of boat propulsion. As previously mentioned, boats in the afterlife are propelled by thought, and practice improves a soul's ability to maneuver and drive them. It is fun to test one's proficiency during contests on the water. It is clearly pointed out, however, that all contests are friendly and offer no prizes to the winner. They take place in an atmosphere without rivalry.

Benson shares insights into how souls in the afterlife experience the "living environment" there, as he addresses the differences in gravity and skill level regarding the typical sports games of Earth:

As most of the outdoor games of the Earth world involve the use of a ball, it will be appreciated that here, where the law of gravity operates under different conditions from yours, anything in the nature of propelling a ball by striking it, would lead to quite hopeless results. I am speaking now of games of a competitive nature.

On the Earth-plane skill in games is acquired by the mastery of the mind over the muscles of the body, when once the latter has been brought to a healthy condition. But here we are always in a healthy condition, and our muscles are always under the complete and absolute control of our minds. Efficiency is quickly gained, whether it is in playing upon a musical instrument, painting a picture, or in any other pursuit that requires the use of the limbs. It will be seen, therefore, that most of the usual games would lose their point here....

It must also be remembered that viewpoints change very much when one comes to live here. What we deemed so very important when we were incarnate, we find is not nearly so important when we arrive in the spirit world. And many of our erstwhile earthly games seem rather tame and trivial beside our greatly increased powers in the spirit world. The fact that we can move ourselves through space instantaneously is enough to make the greatest earthly athletic skill recede into insignificance, and our mundane sports and games are in similar case. Our recreations are more of the mind, and we never feel that we must expend a superfluity of physical energy upon some strenuous action, for

our energy is at a constant level according to our individual re-
quirements. [130]

This certainly brings up an interesting point. If it is true that sports could not be played in the same way in the afterlife, many readers who are especially fond of sports may be very disappointed. If we factor in the idea that "with God all things are possible," an environment featuring the same gravitational qualities as Earth might very well be possible, thus allowing for contests similar to those we have on Earth to take place. But...would they truly be desired?

It is possible that once away from the Earth where egos abound, souls would abandon the desire to "compete" and "win" in these types of contests. An environment of progressively higher states of consciousness and mutual love could very well preclude any desire to engage in competitive sports. It will be interesting to find out!

❧ 37 ❧

Afterlife Grounds

In the Summerland and higher realms all things in the environment are truly ideal, literally perfection in design. There are no roads that are made from concrete or asphalt similar to those on Earth to withstand heavy traffic—there is no heavy traffic. Some reports indicate that beautiful green grass makes up the wide road surfaces, and that it is always perfectly trimmed in height for walking. Smaller paths are surfaced frequently with stone, but the stone has a degree of "springiness" to it. And the colors are more vibrant featuring a great variety of pastel shades.

It is reported that these stones frequently feature designs composed of various materials and colors which all blend in perfectly with their environment. Everything combines to present a feast of color in perfect harmony with the colors of the flowers, the green grass and the blue sky.

Homes are described as being surrounded with lovely lawns, flowers, shrubs, woods, and paths paved with beautiful stone. The natural love of beauty that all souls have is what maintains and even amplifies this beauty, and souls frequently desire to improve this beauty even more. If a particular aspect of the environment becomes the focus of a soul's appreciation of its beauty, it will respond with greater beauty!

❦ 38 ❦

The Soil

The following aspects of the afterlife, namely the soil, the building process, and boundaries have not been addressed by most afterlife reporters, at least not in detail. Monsignor Benson appears to be the only significant source of detailed information regarding these afterlife subjects. He has previously stated that he highly values the importance of describing details. Several researchers have concluded that Benson's reports are logical and believable—his information on more important topics has been in harmony with that of other afterlife reports. Despite such reliance on one source, readers may still find this information interesting, as opposed to not presenting anything on these subjects.

Here is what Monsignor Benson had to say about the makeup of soil in the afterlife:

There is soil, certainly, but it has not the same mineral constituents as that of the Earth-plane, for it must be understood that life here is derived directly from the Great Source. The soil varies in colour and density in different localities in just the same way as upon the Earth-plane....
Firstly, then, it is perfectly dry—I could detect no trace of moisture. I found that it ran off the hand in much the same way that dry sand will do. Its colours vary in a wide range of tones, but never does it approach the dark heavy look of earthly soil. In

some places it is of fine granular formation, while in others it is composed of much coarser particles—that is, relatively coarser.

One of the unexpected properties of this soil is the fact that, while it can be taken into the hand and allowed to run from it smoothly and freely, yet when it is undisturbed it remains fully cohesive, supporting as firmly as the earthly soil all that is growing within it.

The colour of the "earth" is governed by the colour of whatever botanic life it supports. And here again there is no special significance, no deep symbolical reason for this particular order of things. It is simply that the color of the soil is complementary to the colour of the flowers and trees, and the result, which could not be otherwise, is that of inspiring harmony—harmony to the eye, harmony to the mind, and the most soothing musical harmony to the ear. What better reason could there be? And what simpler?[131]

To have soil that changes color to add to the overall color harmony in the environment is another amazing aspect of the afterlife, where every feature is optimized for maximum beauty. Benson also reports that while approaching the lower realms, the soil gradually loses its color and becomes heavier until finally becoming stones and rock. Any remaining grass loses its fresh green color and instead appears to be a dried-out yellow.

Going in the opposite direction toward the higher realms, the soil is described as becoming finer, with more colors and being somewhat translucent. It also provides a greater degree of softness while walking. Every particle appears to have a definite geometric shape. When picked up, this soil flows freely and emits beautiful soft tones, which is similar to what happens while interacting with the water and with flowers.

✣ 39 ✣

The Building Process

Benson reports that a meeting occurs with the higher souls who serve to govern and guide various processes within the realm whenever a new building is to be "constructed." As the need for the building is usually clear and for a good purpose, the formal approval from the ruler is issued in short order.

In the following description, Benson uses the example of an annex to an already existing library, where, periodically, the new books being added require additional space. Not only are new books from the Earth added, but also volumes that were written "solely in spirit," having "no counterpart on Earth." These are written by authorities from the higher realms on the numerous subjects to be found in Creation.

Architects are then consulted, who plan the details of the building. No battle of egos occurs, as all souls in this realm selflessly acknowledge their gifts in humility, and as God-given. They are grateful for the opportunity to humbly and co-operatively provide their individual talents and skills for all fellow souls. Master masons are brought in to help with the construction.

Buildings in the afterlife do not have to have plumbing, electrical, or heating systems, and there is no need for insulation since the outside air temperature is always perfect... windows can be left open! Also, kitchen facilities are not needed.

Benson describes the actual construction of this library annex. Present are the ruler, the masons, architects, and numerous onlookers, all cheerful and in fine spirits:

The act of building in the spirit world is essentially an operation of thought. It will not be surprising, therefore, when I tell you that nowhere were there to be seen the usual materials and paraphernalia associated with earthly builders, the scaffolding and bricks and cement, and the various other familiar objects....

The ruler of the realm stepped forward a few paces, and, with his back towards us, but facing the site upon which the new wing was to arise, he spoke a brief but appropriate prayer. In simple language he asked the Great Creator for His help in the work they were about to undertake.

His prayer brought an instantaneous response, which was in the form of a bright beam of light that descended upon him and upon those gathered immediately behind him. As soon as this happened the architects and masons moved up close beside him.

All eyes were now turned upon that vacant spot beside the main building, to which we noticed that a second beam of light was passing directly from the ruler and the masons. As the second beam reached the site of the annex it formed itself into a carpet of coruscation [emitting sparkling flashes of light] upon the ground. This gradually grew in depth, width, and height, but it seemed, as yet, to lack any suggestion of substance. It matched the main building in colour, but that was all so far.

Slowly the form gained in size until it reached the required height. We could now see plainly that it matched the original structure in general outline, while the carved devices similarly corresponded.[132]

At this point the outline was thoroughly inspected by the architects, inside and out. The building was not solid yet, being more of a tenuous outline. This stage provides ample opportunity to notice any imperfections in the construction and correct them. In this example, no mistakes needed any attention, so the work proceeded:

The downstream of light now became very much more intense, while the horizontal stream from the ruler and his collaborators assumed, after the lapse of a minute or two, a similar degree of intensity. We could now perceive the nebulous form acquiring an unmistakable appearance of solidity as the concentration of united thought laid layer upon layer of increased density upon the simulacrum [image].

From what I observed it seemed to devolve [be delegated] upon the ruler to supply to each of the masons just that quantity and description of force that each required upon his separate task. He acted, in fact, as a distributive agent for the magnetic power that was descending directly upon him. This split up into a number of individual shafts of light of different colour and strength, which corresponded with his direct appeals to the Great Architect. There was no faltering or diminution of the application of thought substance to be perceived anywhere. The masons themselves seemed to work with a complete unanimity of concentration, since the building attained full solidity with a remarkable degree of evenness.[133]

From this point the rays of light were stopped, and the final result of the annex was there in its perfection, exactly matching in color and every detail the original library building.

Benson finishes the subject of building with his comments on the slight differences between building a public building and an individual spirit home for a soul. He cites the "indispensable prerequisite" of home ownership as being the right to own it, earned by the quality of life lived by the soul either while on Earth, or with the increase in that quality since graduating to the afterlife. Once the right to own is earned, the process of building can occur.

He also stated that when it is time for him to leave his own individual spirit home and move on in his spiritual progression, it will be up to him whether to leave it standing for others to use. He reports that the usual custom is to gift one's home to the ruler, allowing him to decide how it will be used.

❧ 40 ❧

Boundaries and Borders
in the Afterlife

Have any of us during our individual earthly sojourn resided in an urban area or other populated place where there were no boundaries, or borders, or fences? Where you and all your neighbors were free to stroll about unrestricted, or more so, welcomed by others wherever you went? This is reported to be the norm in Summerland.

Benson explains how, due to the innate mutual cooperation and respect that is part of the universal spirit of Summerland, there is no fear of trespassing. There exists instead the mutual joy of sharing in the beauty and wonders all around.

I was struck by the fact that there were no signs of walls or hedges or fences; indeed, nothing, so far as I could see, to mark where my garden began or ended. I was told that such things as boundaries were not needed, because each person knew instinctively, but beyond doubt, just where his own garden ended. There was therefore no encroaching upon another's grounds, although all were open to any who wished to traverse them or linger within them.

I was wholeheartedly welcome to go wherever I wished without fear of intruding upon another's privacy. I was told I should find that that was the rule here, and that I would have no

different feelings with respect to others walking in my own gar-
den. It exactly described my sentiments at that moment, for I
wished, then and there, that all who cared would come into the
garden and enjoy its beauties. I had no notions whatever of own-
ership personally, although I knew that it was my own "to have
and to hold." And that is precisely the attitude of all here—own-
ership and partnership at one and the same time.[134]

We are then given a description of a brief foray into the
realms of lower vibration. Benson notes that the land changes
very gradually, and that there is no exact "boundary" line—
rather one level gradually transitions into another. Venturing
towards the lower realms, the turf becomes harder and what
grass remains appears scorched. The flowers, trees, and
homes slowly disappear. No sign of life is present. The temperature is less warm, contributing to a dampness and chill in
the air.

Traveling toward the realms of higher vibration looks
and feels much more inviting. The turf becomes softer, and the
grass radiates a vibrant green. There are more flowers with
more vibrant colors and delightful scents that offered "health-
giving power" that surpassed all previously seen. Beautiful
homes are present, inhabited by souls having made significant
spiritual progress and enjoying frequent contact with the
higher realms. In contrast to the lower realms, here a delightful warmth was present accompanied by a feeling of elation to
be in such a wondrous environment.

After walking forward for a short while Benson and his
group found that they couldn't proceed further. They were not
blocked by any barriers, but they experienced difficulty in
breathing due to the more "rarefied" atmosphere. They were
able to see a few souls, radiating gentle colors, who waved in
a most friendly way, and who seemed to intuitively understand
the purpose of the group's visit and did not approach them.

Although Benson points out that it was the atmosphere
and breathing difficulties that prevented them from continu-

ing, other afterlife sources have stated that it is a higher intensity of vibrations or light that becomes too uncomfortable to bear, making it impossible for a soul not yet at that higher state of soul evolution to remain.

❧ 41 ❧

Aspects of Time

There are numerous afterlife sources reporting a modified sense of time. From the many testimonies of those who have had a near-death experience it appears that the daily measurement of time is somewhat different from how time is recognized here on Earth. NDE'ers report elaborate experiences such as complete life reviews, the exploration of previous lifetimes, travel to other dimensions, and training sessions in afterlife places of learning. And we learn that when the soul of the person experiencing their NDE eventually returns to their body—at the scene of their accident, while traveling in an ambulance or during an emergency hospital operation—that they have usually only been gone for a short period of time. It would seem that the sense of time from the perspective of the afterlife does not correspond entirely with "Earth time."

There are several factors that would tend to alter the sense of time for souls. For one thing, it is reported that there is no night, but only perpetual day. Souls don't experience a night between "days." They live in one perpetual period of natural light, doing whatever their work or chosen service or activity is at that point, until they decide to stop and do another form of work or recreation or another activity. Thus, souls don't need to take a "time out" to sleep or rest, which for us on Earth breaks up every day's activities repeatedly.

Other indications of time that we are used to on Earth include getting hungry and eating. Although there are some testimonies that a soul in the hereafter may eat if they please, they do not need to. In the Summerland and higher realms there is no aging that takes place in the soul body, and no deterioration of physical or mental capabilities. Also, there are no seasons to mark time as we know it—only a continuous summer that souls never stop enjoying.

It has also been reported that there is a degree of awareness of Earth time in keeping with special times on Earth such as Christmas, Easter, and Thanksgiving. Souls often send love and guidance to loved ones on Earth at special times such as birthdays and anniversaries. In general, however, afterlife inhabitants do not mark time in their lives the same way we do.

There have also been a few reports that there is the possibility of everything happening at once! This shocking concept of the simultaneous occurrence of all events is very difficult for most of us to fathom. Those interested in this radical possibility can look to the recent fascinating findings and hypotheses about time, as these are coming forth in cosmology and nuclear physics. Brian Greene in his acclaimed work, *The Fabric of the Cosmos*, published in 2004, is one of a number of twenty-first century physicists who believe they have demonstrated that on a cosmic scale, time is both relative and non-linear. In an experiment described in his book and more recently broadcast in a television program on PBS, Greene claims in a series of remarkable graphics that apply Einstein's theory of relativity to recent discoveries in physics, that all that has occurred or will ever occur, literally all events since the universe took form and proceeding forward to whenever it may cease to be, are all occurring simultaneously![135]

Modern physics contends that our experience of time and the events within the framework of time, are all entirely dependent on our particular placement and our particular orientation and perspective at any given moment. Of course, due to the apparent "presence" of time in our lives, and its "forward progression," this understanding of time is difficult for most to grasp.

One source described this idea of everything happening simultaneously by stating that he could see all events together, and used the analogy that, like marbles in a jar, we could choose to take one out at a time to examine it. Afterlife reports indicate, however, that a sense of time passing still exists. Events occur, then more events occur, and the events follow a sequence.

Though some of these concepts about time may not feel comfortable to many of us, it appears that newly arrived souls adapt easily to any changes in their sense of time passing. And, for our purposes in the near future, this subject of time is one that is relatively less important than our previous subjects pertaining to becoming more spiritual and attuned with God, love, and light. We will very likely need to make our transition to the afterlife before we can fully comprehend how time works.

❦ 42 ❦

What Is it Like to Experience Joy in Heaven?

A spiritual guide through the hand of Reverend Owen comments on receiving the ability to discern what truth is, touching on its joy.

We do not proffer gifts as slaves to princes. But we do come and stand by you with gifts which gold of Earth cannot buy; and to those who are humble and good and of a pure mind we give these gifts of ability to understand the Truth as it is in Jesus, of certain conviction of life beyond and of the joy of it, of fearlessness of disaster here and hereafter, and of companionship and comradeship with angels.[136]

Beyond the pleasures and joys of the Summerland lie the higher realms that contain what many sources agree is the "true Heaven." These higher realms will be addressed in a future book.

Emanuel Swedenborg offers an excellent description of the "heavenly joys" that we shall experience once we learn our lessons and become purified adequately, so that we too can enter the higher and purer realms of Heaven. He believed that very few people know what it is like to experience "heavenly joy." He states that most people think about joy in relation to "external joys," and that they don't feel or know what "inner joy" is.

Scarcely any one at the present day knows what heaven and heavenly joy are....

Man, when he leaves the external or natural man, comes into the internal or spiritual; hence it may be known that heavenly delight is internal and spiritual, not external and natural; and because it is internal and spiritual, that it is purer and more exquisite than natural delight, and that it affects the interiors of man which belong to his soul or spirit....

All delights flow from love; for what a man loves, he feels to be delightful, nor is there delight from any other source.... The delights of the body or the flesh all flow from the love of self and the love of the world.... But the delights of the soul or spirit all flow from love to the Lord and love toward the neighbor, whence also are the affections of good and truth, and interior satisfactions. These loves with their delights flow in from the Lord and from heaven by an internal way, which is from above, and affect the interiors....

Heaven in itself is so full of delights, that, viewed in itself, it is nothing but delight and blessedness... the divine love wills the salvation and happiness of all from inmosts [innermost within the soul] and completely.[137]

Although Swedenborg's writings are several hundred years old, and the language he uses is somewhat different than ours, it remains clear that as we develop our "interior" love of God and others, and while we let the "external" desires for the flesh and worldly goods fade away, we are preparing our soul's ability to give and receive the great blessings from the interior world of spirit.

The delights of heaven are ineffable and likewise innumerable; but innumerable as they are, not one can be known or believed by him who is in the mere delight of the body or the flesh....

It is delightful to all there to communicate their delights and blessings to each other; and because all in the heavens are of this character, it is obvious how immense is the delight of heaven....

Such communication flows from the two loves of heaven, which, as was said, are love to the Lord and love toward the neighbor; and it is the nature of these loves to communicate their delights. Love to the Lord is of this nature, because the Lord's love is the love of communicating all that He has to all His creatures, for He wills the happiness of all; and a similar love is in each of those who love Him, because the Lord is in them. Hence there is with the angels [souls] a mutual communication of their delights to each other....

The love of self withdraws and takes away all delight from others, and directs it to itself, for it wishes well to itself alone; and the love of the world wishes that what is the neighbor's were its own. Wherefore these loves are destructive of delights with others. If they are communicative, it is for the sake of themselves, and not for the sake of others....

Love to the Lord and love toward the neighbor wish to communicate all their own to others, for this is their delight; and the love of self and of the world wish to take from others what belongs to them, and to appropriate it to themselves.[138]

Swedenborg makes such an important point here. It is important for each person to reduce and eventually shed the love of the base and non-beautiful things on Earth, so that they can at the same time develop their natural love of taking delight in loving others and God, which brings indescribable interior feelings of bliss. When we do this, we are destined to experience deep and profound inner joy as we travel onward beyond the Earth and into eternal life. There, many of the external "trappings" that we associate with joy here on Earth (a fancy home, money, and the "baubles and trinkets" of human life) are not necessary. Instead, we experience the joys of the spirit that move us to our very core—our pure inner being that is so closely related to and really, one with God. We can anticipate a strong and new quality of joy in our eternal destiny.

It is vital to remember the importance of light—how focusing, meditating, visualizing and *feeling* divine light can be of significant help in the education and uplifting of the soul, bringing feelings of peace and calm. Light, along with keeping life's divine purposes of goodness, beauty, and love in mind, can lift us above the fear, stress, and confusion that are the daily fare of millions of souls on Earth.

Having light in one's consciousness helps us transmute any frustrations in our lives or in our personalities, and brings us closer to the reality of divine love. Meditating on light is a beautiful experience.

The following powerful meditation, if practiced regularly, will result in wonderful blessings of light:

The first step to the control of yourself—is the stilling of all outer activity—of both mind and body. Fifteen to thirty minutes— at night before retiring and in the morning before beginning the day's work—using the following exercise—will do wonders for anyone—who will make the necessary effort.

For the second step, make certain of being undisturbed, and after becoming very still—picture and feel your body enveloped in a Dazzling White Light. The first five minutes—while holding this picture—recognize—and feel intensely—the connection between the outer self and Your Mighty God Within—focusing your attention upon the heart center—and visualizing it—as a Golden Sun.

The next step is the acknowledgment—"I now joyously accept—the Fullness of the Mighty God Presence—the Pure Christ." Feel—the Great Brilliancy of the Light and intensify It—in every cell of your body for at least ten minutes longer.

Then close the meditation by the command, "I am a Child of the Light—I Love the Light—I Serve the Light—I Live in the Light—I am Protected, Illumined, Supplied, Sustained by the Light, and I Bless the Light."[139]

The above meditation was reportedly given to us by the Ascended Master known as Saint Germain, through the hand of his earthly amanuensis (one who takes dictation), Godfrey Ray King. Results will be experienced if it is practiced regularly. The following comments about light were also given right after the meditation itself:

Remember always, "One becomes that upon which he meditates," and since all things have come forth from the Light, Light is the Supreme Perfection and Control of all things.

Contemplation and adoration of the Light compels Illumination to take place in the mind—health, strength, and order to come into the body—and peace, harmony, and success to manifest in the affairs of every individual—who will really do it, and seeks to maintain it.

All the way down the centuries—in every age, under every condition—we are told by all who have expressed the greater accomplishments of Life that—the Light is Supreme—the Light is everywhere—and in the Light—exist all things.[140]

Throughout the above, the word "light" was originally in quotes, to denote that it meant that it is the Kingdom of God—God's Consciousness—the original source and Creator of all.

PEACE AND JOY
TO ALL SOULS OF GOODWILL!

PART III

QUESTIONS AND MISCONCEPTIONS ABOUT THE AFTERLIFE

❧ 43 ❧

Is There Absolute "Proof" of an Afterlife?

From the dawn of human history, the earnest pursuit to understand all of the many aspects of the mystery of existence, of life itself, has persisted. This has led to the appearance of shamans, mystics, wise men, and priests, and their rituals, insights, teachings, and doctrines that attempt to fill the great void of understanding. These insights provide souls on their earthly sojourn with a measure of comfort, a sense of security, and a degree of guidance pertaining to the areas of human existence that lie beyond practical daily affairs and material science in general.

Nearly all of the great philosophers from Plato to the present time have expressed, in one form or another, varied theories as to the realm of existential, supernatural and cosmological phenomena that are difficult to prove beyond any doubt, because of the clear and indisputable limits of human perception. Many of these philosophers and spiritual leaders also believe in a spiritual existence within us that composes the eternal part of our soul that is more real than our physical form, which undergoes constant change.

Individuals must discover their own proof as a product of individual effort—derived from one's own love of God, research, and also prayer and meditation. What seems abundantly clear is that a new world of spirituality is coming for each one of us, even for those who only believe in what they can see and who do not discover an "afterlife" until after leaving their life on Earth.

It is a universal spiritual law that the individual has free will! No soul can truly embrace a concept or characteristic about God or the Creation unless this is done without any pressure from outside sources. We learn from Sister Frances Banks that in the afterlife:

No acceptance of another soul's belief colors progress. The soul must judge for itself—must make its own progress, must choose what to accept as truth for itself. No soul is coerced, forced or bound by creeds.[141]

The power of transformational change lies in the individual's desire to learn. Knowledge increases belief, which turns into *knowing,* which empowers change. It increases the motivation to focus on God, spiritual reality, truth, and righteous living.

Many people are afraid to accept their spirituality. For some, this is caused by their fear of the unknown. Individuals choose not to think about it, to indulge in a sort of psychological avoidance, "whatever will be, will be." Some believe that they have sinned so much that their afterlife experience will be eternal suffering. But our God is merciful and forgiving. There is no eternal suffering, because most stubborn souls who are self-centered and have caused great suffering for others eventually acknowledge God, make amends, and forgive others and themselves. Some make choices to live in their own world, which blocks their spiritual growth. It is only the most vicious and cruel souls who have created an extreme load of karma by turning away from God completely, causing continual and great amounts of suffering, who have their energies literally 'returned to God.'

It is quite reassuring to *know,* to have absolute certainty, that a beautiful afterlife awaits nearly all people. Countless thousands of people who have had near-death experiences have received proof of an afterlife. Most of these people have returned invigorated to finish their Earth lives with significantly greater enthusiasm, joy and spirituality. Other people, including myself, have been blessed with proof of an afterlife due to personal spiritual experiences we have had while here on Earth and in our waking consciousness. Still others come to believe through an extensive analysis of the abundant amounts of afterlife data, such as are cited in this book.

It is difficult for open-minded readers, once exposed to this evidence, to deny the existence of an afterlife. For souls who strongly believe it does *not* exist, they should pose themselves the question, "Am I truly being an open-minded individual, or is my skepticism, even though it is logical to have skepticism, so great that it is blocking me from deeper insights?"

Those who desire a detailed reporting of the varied categories of afterlife evidence can read Victor Zammit's *A Lawyer Presents the Evidence for the Afterlife.* Anyone who thoroughly researches this topic with an open mind will discover that the reality of the afterlife is beyond doubt and needs no more evidence than we already have.

~ 44 ~

Do We Experience the Loss of Individuality?

T he scariest idea for some people who contemplate where we ultimately wind up is the idea of losing one's individuality when we get to the stage of becoming "One with our Creator." There are certainly many afterlife sources that speak about becoming more "at-one" with God and all of life. But as this occurs, we are informed again and again that a soul's sense of self expands to include this "allness." The flow of light increases and awareness expands in whatever direction a soul chooses to focus. Instead of feeling a loss of self, we all have the potential to experience a significantly larger "gain of self."

Silver Birch, a spirit guide who spoke through Maurice Barbanell, addresses this concern about loss of individuality. The message here is incredibly uplifting:

All spiritual progress is toward increasing individuality. You do not become less of an individual. You become more of an individual. You develop latent gifts, you acquire great knowledge, your character becomes stronger, more of the divine is exhibited through you.... What you succeed in doing is finding yourself.[142] [Emphasis added.]

Emanuel Swedenborg also confirms our ongoing individuality:

Almost all who enter the other life suppose that every one is in the same hell, or in the same heaven; when yet there are infinite varieties and diversities in both. The hell of one is never precisely like that of another, nor is the heaven of one exactly the same as the heaven of another; just as no man, spirit, or angel is ever exactly like another, even as to the face. When I only thought that two might be exactly alike or equal, the angels were astonished, saying that every whole is formed by the harmonious agreement of many parts, and that the character of the whole is according to that agreement.[143]

As we focus more and more on God, love, and light, we become more and more of these aspects of our Creator! And in this "cosmic process," we find ourselves coming closer to knowing the Will of God. We lose the desire to follow the will of our lower/ego-driven self, and naturally embrace the higher divine wisdom. We will indeed come to experience a loss of the individuality of our lower self, the self that is not our ultimate real divine self. But this is a great blessing, as that ego-driven self is error-prone and the cause of so much human suffering. Various higher sources state that our divine Christ Self and I AM Presence are unique, indicating eternal individuality within the Oneness of the All. Perhaps, ultimately, we expand our self to incorporate and join with all other souls and all other things. If that is the case, nothing will be lost, there will only be gain.

Here we are reminded again from Sacred Scripture, whereby we learn in First Corinthians that:

One star differeth from another star in glory.[144]

❦ 45 ❦

Are We All Alone, Without Help?

There is never a lack of help from other souls if there is a need for help. The desire to serve others is the primary motive for action in the afterlife, as well as the essence of our true divine nature. This is love and kindness in action, within the nature of the very light that is pouring into our souls, within the consciousness of every soul at the levels of the Summerland and higher.

Help, assistance, companionship and guidance—all of these are available for every soul. Sometimes we are helped without asking, while other times it is necessary to ask. This is true for all of us here on Earth, as well as for souls in the afterlife.

❧ 46 ❧

Are We Issued Angel Wings?

Some fans of the delightful movie classic, *It's a Wonderful Life,* might wonder if, like the endearing angel Clarence, angels in Heaven are issued "angel wings." But we learn that in the heaven world, angels don't need wings to fly or to transport themselves from place to place. The following excerpt from Julia Ames reveals reasons why souls who minister to those on Earth sometimes display themselves as having wings.

> *The Angel Guardian who came to me had wings.... It is not usual, but if we please we can assume them. They are no more necessary than any of the contrivances by which you attempt to attain the mastery of the spirit over the burden of matter. We think and we are there. Why, then, wings? They are scenic illusions useful to convey the idea of superiority to earth-bound conditions, but we do not use them any more than we use steam-engines. But I was glad my Guide had wings. It seemed more like what I thought it would be, and I was at once more at ease than I would otherwise have been.*[145]

Julia was comforted, immediately after her transition to the afterlife, by seeing an angel with wings. The wings conveyed to her that things were different now, that she was safe and would be guided. She also states how in her later role of helping others she could display wings, for the same good purpose of immediately showing spiritual help was at hand for others in need of that help.

❧ 47 ❧

Isn't the Afterlife Empty, Shadowy, Even Plain and Dreary?

There are some people on Earth who may ridicule descriptions of an afterlife that contain such beauty that has been described within these pages. They may not believe in the truly "heavenly countryside," with the transcendent flowers and trees, lakes and rivers, habitations and fulfilling work and leisure activities.

Because of limited, earthbound fantasies, they might more easily believe in ghosts with little intelligence, surviving in dimly lit areas of gloom and disconnected from anything that was happy or pleasant on Earth. They are unable to believe in having an active soul body with limitless energy. They believe that all the goodness of life is confined only to the Earth world—that the Earth is superior to every other world!

This somewhat prevalent, but patently false belief, may be the reason why deep sympathy is felt for people who leave the Earth and must travel to this supposed land of gloom and emptiness, leaving behind all the beauty of the Earth. Many people mistakenly believe that worthwhile, fulfilling things to do can only be done on Earth. This is why souls who believe this way are shocked when they awaken to the next chapter in their soul's onward progression. This is often when a greater sense of humility occurs. These souls never receive reproach, except sometimes from themselves.

In the afterlife, souls are sooner or later filled with gratitude to our Creator. The beautiful environment is a constant reminder of the divine love and the grace bestowed upon every humble soul.

Monsignor Benson offers a humorous (it's "very unhealthy" to be dead!) opinion of Earth dwellers who believe that living on Earth is the best, and that after our transition, life is awful.

It is customary among certain minds of the Earth to regard the spirit world and its inhabitants as vague and shadowy, extremely unsubstantial and speculative. These same minds regard the dwellers in spirit lands as a class of sub-human beings who are immeasurably worse off than themselves simply because they are 'dead.' To be upon Earth is normal, sound, and healthy, and infinitely to be preferred. To be 'dead' is unfortunate but, of course, inevitable, very unhealthy, and anything but normal. The 'dead' are much to be pitied because they are not alive on Earth. This line of thought tends to place an undue importance upon the earthly life and upon the physical body of man. It is as though it were only at the point of 'death' that man takes upon himself any spiritual nature, whereas, in truth, that spiritual nature has been present within him since the moment of his drawing his first breath upon Earth.[146]

Benson makes the important point that we on Earth are already fully equipped with our spiritual nature, even if it is somewhat dormant, and even if we are unaware of its full potential. As has been reported earlier, our spiritual bodies interpenetrate our physical bodies and are what we utilize after leaving behind our physical body.

It appears as though material things are provided in stages beyond Earth life as stepping stones. Various afterlife sources acknowledge and attempt to describe how experiences become more subjective and less objective as a soul evolves to higher levels. Despite being more subjective, it is reported that these spiritual levels are more real, because there, life is closer to the spiritual source of all. We are gradually weaned from the physical world with its illusory objectivity. Over time we do get used to a less physical but more spiritually real existence.

Based on the research of Zammit, Crookall, and others, in God's magnificent Creation there are clearly realms following upon realms, and reality extending to infinity, suggesting to us that, as our souls evolve, we will be experiencing and growing with ever-new wonders of the Creation forevermore.

Eye hath not seen, nor ear heard, neither have entered into the heart of man, the things which God hath prepared for them that love him.[147]

⚜ 48 ⚜

In the End, Is the Afterlife Simply Boring?

It is reassuring to know that the afterlife is filled with numerous opportunities to engage in interesting activities—work and service helping others, ever new possibilities for learning and for joyous and fulfilling recreation, and even rest and reflection when needed.

As has been touched upon earlier, many on Earth who believe in an afterlife also believe that it consists of singing hymns and saying prayers all the time. What we have seen instead is that there is much useful activity in addition to singing and praying. In fact, it may be asserted with confidence that the potential for engaging in meaningful and inspiring service, all for the progression of the greater good, is quite literally limitless.

Souls are never bored. If a soul begins to experience a sense of boredom, they are led to take the next step in their progression; they might take a well-needed break or move on to a new form of helpful and useful service. The Summerland and beyond are unlimited worlds, and souls can be continually conscious of the Creator of our Universe, since the evidence is everywhere.

Although there is rest available for souls who need it, the afterlife is not at all a place of "eternal rest," as that phrase is often used on Earth. Whenever any needed rest is completed, the desire to be up and doing useful service of some sort returns to inspire and uplift the soul once again.

❦ 49 ❧

What About Certain Orthodox Religious Teachings?

C ertain tenets within orthodox religion are man-made. Again and again this is made clear by those who visit the afterlife through near-death experiences and by souls communicating from afterlife realms. What so often is asserted in orthodox doctrine does not always mesh with the truth of what our God-given universe is really all about.

To give one example, a common doctrine within some orthodox teachings holds that repentance made on one's deathbed may have great value. A great deal of afterlife testimony indicates that this is not so. Although it would have a degree of value, depending on its level of sincerity, that deathbed act does not replace the need for the subsequent life review which enables a greater understanding and empathy concerning those who were harmed. During his or her life review a soul comes to appreciate both the successes and the failures of their earthly sojourn, both the good they brought forth and the pain and suffering they may have caused.

The state of consciousness of any particular soul is not suddenly transformed upon entering the afterlife. The soul's character is very much rooted in the level of comprehension developed up to the time of transition to the next world.

Nor does any deathbed repentance substitute for any amends that may be required, as discussed in the earlier chapter on judgment. It is then that souls can begin to reform and to move on. In most, but not all cases, a soul will be strongly motivated to overcome their shortcomings, make amends, and evolve in the beautiful healing and transformative afterlife our loving Creator has prepared for us.

Religious creeds are not the law in the afterlife. Many, though well intended, are completely untrue. Only spiritual and universal law apply, and the gist of God's eternal law is the Golden Rule:

Therefore all things whatsoever ye would that men should do to you: do ye even so to them: for this is the law and the prophets.[148]

Free will is always honored in the afterlife. No attempts are made to coerce souls to believe a particular doctrine. Religious communities do exist, and some do retain some elements of their ongoing prejudices, which serve to limit practicing souls. Facts may be presented to souls, but they have freedom to reject or accept them.

After sufficient exposure to the truth of afterlife reality, souls evolve by freeing themselves of whatever dogma does not fit with the greater truths that become progressively more apparent as they share in the many blessings of the hereafter.

❧ 50 ❧

Visiting Gravesites

It is questionable whether people on Earth should visit the graves of loved ones repeatedly, especially if each time they are still filled with an intense sense of loss and a longing for the departed. Visiting gravesites can encourage the visitors to begin a stream of depressing thoughts that are focused on the departed soul, which could create a drawing influence on that soul from those sorrowful thoughts being sent their way. Weaker departed souls might be unable to resist this drawing influence back to the location of their discarded physical body—which can actually cause a big distraction and keep them from their spiritual advancement.

It is fine, however, to visit a grave on occasion and send strong and positive thoughts and prayers to the departed— loving thoughts for their continuing on in their journey of life, and joyous anticipation of a grand reunion in the afterlife. Of course, it is also true that this can be done from anywhere, not necessarily just from their gravesite.

Generally, afterlife messages and testimonials confirm that it is best to avoid, whether at a gravesite or at home, a prolonged inordinate grieving process. The sooner those left behind can accept their loss and send positive thoughts to the departed, the sooner the departed soul can be "cut free," so that no strong desire to return to Earth holds them back.

There is a grieving process, and it has a start and a finish. Those needing help during this difficult time can receive support from local bereavement groups and from counseling. The best kind of support is the listening ear of a loving friend.

Hopefully, everyone who reads this book will realize that learning more about the afterlife is a tremendous help in avoiding prolonged grief over the departure of a loved one. It is also wonderful to look forward to the joyous reunions with loved ones that will occur once we have made our own transition!

⁓ 51 ⁓

What Is the Status
of Famous People in the Afterlife?

In the afterlife, fame is very different from fame on Earth. In fact, after a soul passes into the afterlife, "fame" in the sense that we would understand the term here on Earth, is only gained through rendering service to other souls. The law of *cause and effect* applies to all equally. Some souls who were famous on Earth for honorable service to others proceed to higher realms to continue their good work. Other souls who were likewise well known on Earth, but whose works were not for the good of humanity, may reside in the lower realms for quite some time.

From the broader perspective, souls, whether they were famous or not on Earth, arrive at the destination which closely conforms to: their state of consciousness, the development of their heart, the type of service they have rendered while on Earth, their religious and ideological convictions, and the level which fits with their likes and dislikes. But preeminently, it is their spiritual worth that determines their new afterlife location. What they actually accomplished on Earth to help others is what counts the most!

Discretion is practiced in the spirit world. The life that a soul led on Earth is private to themselves, unless the soul feels ready to share life experiences with others. Souls learn not to ask prying questions of others, including famous persons, after they have passed over, unless the newly arrived soul initiates the subject. If that occurs, there are always compassionate souls who will listen.

In the Summerland, all souls realize that they are individual parts of a whole, a vast, virtually infinite organization of Life. All souls in this grand web are united in their efforts for ongoing spiritual development and progress.

The relative value of the honors and accumulations of wealth and power achieved on Earth is extremely low compared to the potential spiritual riches that can be achieved in the afterlife. And the spirit world environment makes for a "level playing field" where all have equal opportunity.

We have learned that the "riches" in the afterlife can include the right to have your own home. The riches are also comprised of the greater beauty found on each succeeding "higher" level as a soul progresses. More importantly, they consist of greater love and gratitude to God, greater mutual love and respect shared with others, the ever-expanding inner joy of helping others in need, and the ongoing, never-ending process of experiencing and learning about the wonders of Creation.

PART IV

KEYS FOR SPIRITUAL ATTUNEMENT

⚜ 52 ⚜

Many Have Forgotten
Who They Really Are

Many have forgotten that we are spirit, temporarily inhabiting a physical form. We have forgotten that God is within us, is omnipresent in all things and that we are His divine sons and daughters.

Dr. Melvin Morse, voted three times one of "America's Best Doctors," and author of the best-selling *Closer to the Light,* concluded from his research that only in the past few centuries has mankind lost their awareness of the spirit within and of life after death. For that reason, we now have a significant and unnatural fear of death that blocks our ability to fully live life.[149]

Betty Eadie reports that during her near-death experience she learned that we are not native to this planet, but that being in physical form is our opportunity to learn mastery over the challenges of the flesh.

The Earth is not our natural home...we did not originate here. I was gratified to see that the Earth is only a temporary place for our schooling and that sin is not our true nature.... Although our spirit bodies are full of light, truth, and love, they must battle constantly to overcome the flesh, and this strengthens them. Those who are truly developed will find a perfect harmony between their flesh and spirits, a harmony that will bless them with peace and give them the ability to help others.[150]

While we are on Earth, there is, for most of us, certainly room for improvement in maintaining a high, pure, and positive quality of thinking. Let us remember, however, that here on Earth, we have to deal with *a lot* of negativity. It is far easier in the Summerland to avoid negative thoughts because there, where everyone and everything is beautiful and there are no concerns about money or health, souls can feel love in the very atmosphere. In this regard, living on Earth gives us a greater opportunity to master our thinking—here on Earth is where we are tested in our patience with others, and our ability to forgive.

It is so comforting to realize our true identity in spirit, to *know* we have an eternal afterlife awaiting us upon leaving our physical bodies. We are here to experience the many challenges and temptations that exist on Earth, and to develop our mastery over them. What helps us immensely in overcoming all challenges on Earth is remembering that we are truly eternal spirit. Judge David Patterson Hatch, who died in 1912, addresses this through the hand of Elsa Barker:

If you could only get hold of the idea of immortal life and cling to it! If you could realize yourself as being without beginning and without end, then you might commence to do things worthwhile. It is a wonderful consciousness, that consciousness of eternity. Small troubles seem indeed small to him who thinks of himself in the terms of a million years. You may make the figure a billion, or whatever you like, but the idea is the same.[151]

When we are aware of the truth of our eternality, we feel free to live a full life. We then realize the importance of doing things that are of benefit to others in a grand application of the Golden Rule, for that is indeed what is behind the goodness of God and Heaven. We can experience the glorious awareness, the joy of God's presence in the form of Divine Light and Love, permeating all.

❦ 53 ❦

The Importance
of Our Self-Image

It is vitally important to include our Higher/Real/Divine Self in our self-image. This chapter contains a few excerpts from my previous book, *Unifying Truths of the World's Religions*, on this crucial topic.

There is one underlying cause for the needless tragedy, suffering, fighting and lack in the world. It is simply this: *mankind has an identity crisis.*

Because we have forgotten that we are truly spirit, temporarily inhabiting a physical form, we are vulnerable to all kinds of fear, stress, misunderstandings, jealousies, and a host of other negatives.

The importance of knowing our true identity cannot be over-emphasized. When we forget that we are ultimately one with God, and with our fellow man, we get into trouble. We need to remember that divinity lies in everyone, though it must be said that in some, its light has been totally eclipsed. If we would make spiritual progress, it is imperative that we practice *seeing* and *knowing* that divinity.

The self-image that we each have of ourselves is crucial to how we treat ourselves, as well as how we treat others and, not least, how we treat God. One of the universal concepts in the many modalities of psychological practice is the understanding of how essential a positive self-image is for happiness and mental balance. For most of us, life fluctuates between Heaven and Hell depending on our closeness with spirit and how well we forgive ourselves and others. Each of us needs to discover, remember, and earnestly apply the truth of our divinity.[152]

Dannion Brinkley, after having two near-death experiences, was able at times to read other people's thoughts. In his book, *At Peace in the Light,* he writes about how so many people have a poor self-image.

I was amazed by how negatively people viewed themselves. I still am.... They all seemed to feel guilty about something or other that they had done in their lives. Many felt they had done wrong things in their lives or that life had beaten them down so much that they felt inferior. I could tell that they never allowed themselves to touch themselves spiritually. Instead, they focused on the surface things in their lives and picked themselves apart. Person after person, I could hear them think that they were ugly, overweight, or poor, or bad parents, or just downright dumb....

Rarely did the people whose thoughts I was picking up focus on what great and powerful spiritual beings they were. Few took credit for their greatness.... They see themselves as being trapped in a reality that is controlled and manipulated by everybody else. I often wondered how much the system had to do with their low self-opinions—institutions from government to religion are always expressing people's inadequacy. And amazingly, people seem to accept that judgment.... They felt unimportant, as though they were just cogs in the machine of society.[153]

Our self-image is constantly reinforced, for good or ill, by our self-talk. In the field of psychology, it is generally acknowledged that how we treat others is just like our inner self-talk! We should pause many times a day to remind ourselves who we really are.

We are a part of God. We are spirit. But we are not only a part of God, as objects of His Creation; no, we are much more; we are in fact His offspring, His very children, His sons and daughters! Not only does the Bible and all the major sacred texts from the world religions confirm this, but also the broad consensus of afterlife data confirms this.

Some may think, "That sounds terrific. But why am I not happier, and why is there so much suffering in this world?" The answer, of course, is that God gave us free will. God has free will, and as we are His offspring and, literally, made "in His image and likeness," we too possess free will. God gave us free will because He loves His children. He loves us and wants His Divine Family to co-create with Him in ever more glorious goodness, beauty and joy.

Just as a child makes a lot of mistakes while learning to walk, we also make mistakes as we learn to perfect ourselves in all areas of life. And when errors occur, suffering occurs. This is simply the reality of life. But what is forgotten or misinterpreted by many belief systems is that it is possible to perfect ourselves.

We might then ask, "How can that be?" when reflecting on numerous past sins or errors. After all, although God Almighty is perfect; how can we humans be perfect too?

It is important to understand that the *real you* is perfect. The *real you* was created by God, and God can only create perfection. And God has qualities that would make it impossible for Him to be separate from the *real you*. Among God's aspects are omnipresence, omniscience and omnipotence. Thus, it would be impossible for God to not be within the *real you*.

Each one of us is a being equipped with awareness—with a vital consciousness that can be 100 percent attuned to God and His many blessings. The pure, good and true aspect of every person is a part of the all-encompassing, omnipresent consciousness of our Creator. This part is the *real you*.

We can also choose to ignore God or be poorly attuned with God. We can hold many false beliefs and even feel a great sense of separateness from God, from others or even from ourselves, and again, especially from our own Real Self.

We may call the perfect, divine, and eternal part of ourselves our Higher or Divine Self. We may call the imperfect non-eternal part of ourselves our unreal or lower-self. The imperfect, human aspects of us are not divine, not perfect and not eternal.

When we create negatives such as hatred, greed, or jealousy, we are still using God's energy (which all energy is), but not in accordance with God's will for good. We are removed from God to the degree that we have chosen to think, act, and feel in ways that are not of God.

The unreal self is the product of our free will. We are not our unreal self with its imperfections. Our imperfections are baggage that weighs us down. But this weight can be lightened and eliminated. As we gradually change the negative aspects contained in our unreal selves, we move closer to our authentic self and become more "real." We can attune more readily to Divine Wisdom and Divine Love, which then allows access to more Divine Power/Light/Energy.

God's will is always perfect. Doing God's will makes one happy and content—if not immediately, eventually. As we focus on the many positive God qualities in our lives (such as peace, love, kindness, mercy, forgiveness and wisdom) we become more of our True/Divine Self. Focusing on God/Light helps us to shed more of the unreal aspects of self that consist of ego, illusion and negativity. We are co-creators *with* God every moment we qualify His energy for good. Every moment we qualify His energy unwisely we are still creating, but not with God's blessing or will.

We are God incarnate, in the sense that we can co-create using God's energy. For many people, ignorance caused by their unreal self blocks the awareness of this. Each one of us needs to discover, remember and apply the truth of our divinity, *anchoring our Higher Self into our self-image!*[154]

There are additional influences on our self-talk, how we treat others and how we develop as well as change our self-image. Julia Ames, from her perspective in the afterlife, touches on other influences on our thoughts. Some may be part of our "larger self" but not known to our consciousness, while others may be from different souls.

The Guardian Angel is indeed a kind of other self, a higher, purer, and more developed section of your own personality. This is perhaps a little difficult to understand, but it is true. There are, as well as good, evil angels, who are with us no less constantly, and they are also sometimes visible as Angels of Darkness when we come across them. They are with us always, and we are with them here when we leave our bodies. We are always swaying hither and thither towards our good and evil guides. We call them, or we did call them, impulses, wayward longings, aspirations, coming we know not where or whence. We see on this side where they come from.[155]

Although Miss Ames states the "Angels of Darkness" are always with us, they are largely unable to continue their negative attempts to influence us once we have reached the levels beyond the Summerland. The point here is that there are many negative influences that we have to overcome from various sources to achieve our freedom. Once we reach a certain degree of success in denying any particular negative influence, we will not be bothered by it further. We have overcome and mastered that particular habit, tendency or temptation to misuse our energy.

We need to view ourselves, and our self-image, in a realistic way that includes our divinity, our real divine self! Some teachings refer to this as our Mighty "I AM Presence," and "Holy Christ Self," the "Christ" defined as the archetype of God's son, the intermediary between God and man. Whatever we want to call it, we are an eternal consciousness that is a part of God, of the All. The more we operate from an awareness and attunement with that, the greater our life experience will be.

One of several ways that we can do this is to regularly monitor our thoughts. It's important to know when our negative/unreal self is dominating our thoughts. Our conscience, which is an aspect of our Divine Self, enables us to distinguish right from wrong. This ability can be blocked by focusing on past or present negatives. Applying the principles of goodness and right living from these insights from the afterlife, as well as those held in common by the world's religions, clears the way so our Divine Self can clearly communicate with us.

Whenever we think and act for the good, we allow another portion of our unreal self to fade away. And, of course, when we do this we are simultaneously strengthening our bond to the Divine Light within.

Our essential self is our consciousness, which is not dependent on a physical body. When our current physical body has been shed, we will be less encumbered in our ability to see the real, spiritual world, where our Real Self, in the truest sense, has always been dwelling.

Incorporating the concept of our Higher/Divine Self into our self-image is a key component to our Divine Vision. This is discussed in the following chapter.

Let us not forget God's love for us in doing this. A simple affirmation, such as "The Love of God is with me NOW" can help to include God's love in our life experience. Once felt, that divine love can be freely given to others, creating a beautiful flow from its infinite supply.

All communications that have come to us from the "Higher Realms" of the afterlife stress the point that "Life is a chance to love," as John said in the Bible.

If we love one another, God dwelleth in us and His love is perfected in us.[156]

As we incorporate the above perfect, loving, and divine aspects into our self-image, it might be helpful to be reminded of the following quotation. It is from Thomas Troward (1847–1916), past president of the International New Thought Alliance, a lecturer on mental science, and whose philosophy inspired the breakthrough bestseller, "The Secret."

My mind is a center of Divine operation. The Divine operation is always for expansion and fuller expression, and this means the production of something beyond what has gone before, something entirely new, not included in the past experience, though proceeding out of it by an orderly sequence of growth.[157]

👈 54 👉

Divine Vision
Makes All the Difference

What we *believe* can play a very important role in our initial afterlife experience. At the time of this writing, Google shows 154,000,000 hits for "the power of belief." There have been numerous studies that prove the impact of a person's belief regarding what they experience. Keep in mind this power as the driving force behind creating and maintaining your perfect vision. From the Bible's Proverbs, we have:

Where there is no vision, the people perish: but he that keepeth the law, happy is he.[158]

And from Napoleon Hill, author of the bestselling *Think and Grow Rich*, we have:

Whatever the mind of man can conceive and believe it can achieve.[159]

We humans, by nature, *need* something good to believe in, something that makes our lives worth living and that gives us meaning and purpose. And, by God's wonderful grace, *we have it!* So many souls on Earth are in despair, trapped in a narrow little room of consciousness, and not knowing the magnificent and awesome truth of our divine and eternal lives.

Joseph Campbell, American mythologist and scholar of comparative religion, referred to humanity's "collective lack of spiritual vision" as the breeding ground for many of society's ailments. We must not forget that how we live our lives here on Earth has tremendous importance for our future in the afterlife. He also said:

> The conquest of the fear of death is the recovery of life's joy.[160]

Divine Vision makes all the difference because having it will *revitalize* us, it will *re-energize* us, producing streams of *loving energy* through us, filled with *loving emotion* (energy in motion). It enables us to live life with the fire of truth, the fire of hope, and will regenerate all those who hold to this higher spiritual Vision of their ultimate reason for being.

We were not created by our Loving Father to be fearful—but to be victorious in the light of Cosmic Truth. We are meant to experience joy in this Light and Truth, to dispel the illusions and the now-prevalent apathy, hopelessness, and cynicism due to the false belief that there is nothing worthwhile to believe in.

We can be, if we choose, just like the seemingly lost soul who gazes upward, as in the old saying, "Two men looked out through prison bars, one saw mud, the other stars."

The truth can be found by those who are ready to receive it. As Divine Sons and Daughters of God, we are meant to have victory over all death and darkness!

When we strengthen our spiritual vision and knowledge, we will create a significant contribution to the uplifting of Earth. Starting every day with a clear vision of *who we really are* and the noble goals we have set for ourselves, with a strong knowledge of why we desire them to be met, will surely guide us toward achieving a productive and successful life. Every day can then be spent taking us closer to those goals.

Let us remember some of the basic facts of life:

1) We are spirits, temporarily inhabiting a physical form. We quite literally are spirit, not matter!

2) It is important for every soul to not overly identify with the physical body.

3) There is far, far more to life than what our earthly eyes can see or perceive.

4) There is a life awaiting us which is, by far, more real and tangible and fulfilling than this Earth life.

5) What we do in this lifetime on Earth, how we conduct ourselves, how we treat other people and all parts of Life has tremendous value for our future in eternity.

6) There is SO MUCH to look forward to in the future! This life should be a joyful anticipation of our next life!

7) GOD IS WITHIN US! A part of God our Creator is living inside of us, and endures after our material existence ceases.

Neither shall they say, Lo here! Or, lo there! For, behold, the Kingdom of God is within you.[161]

No matter the challenges in this world, if we can do two things, we will be sustained and inspired to continue on. First, we can focus on and operate from our true and divine Higher Self that allows the natural flow of love and forgiveness to enfold all in our world. Second, we can create and maintain our Divine Vision. The life after this earthly life will be freer, more beautiful, and more loving if we do. The kind of person we are today will determine what environment we'll find ourselves in and the kind of souls we shall be with in the afterlife.

It is important that our Divine Vision include the following:

1) An accurate self-image of who we really are: Divine Sons and Daughters of God.

2) A strong belief/knowing that God is real.

3) A strong belief/knowing that life is eternal, that Heaven awaits all good and decent people. (We don't have to be perfect, but we must be sincerely striving for goodness.)

4) The noble and loving goals we have set for ourselves, with a strong knowledge of why we desire them to be met. Every day can then be spent taking us closer to those goals.

❧ 55 ❧

Now Is the Time—
A Very Exciting and Intense Time!

December 21, 2012, the end of the Mayan calendar, marked the beginning of a new cycle. Contrary to popularized interpretations predicting massive changes on that day, that date simply marked the beginning of a new era in cosmological and human history. We have Mother Mary's prophecies, Jonathan Cahn's *The Harbinger* and *The Mystery of the Shemitah*, the Zoroastrian prophecies, the Hindu Kali Yuga, the Incan prophecy, the Hopi prophecy, and others. They all say that *now* is a very special time. More information about these prophecies can be researched on the internet.

According to Cahn's *The Harbinger*, God has allowed certain protections to be removed in order that we may be shaken awake—awakened to the reality of our dependence on God, and the importance of righteous living instead of society's current focus on less honorable pursuits. There is always room for a closer relationship with God, and the present era is a special time for that—a time when that closer relationship will be strongly needed.

Throughout history, periods of enlightenment have been accompanied by darkness pushing in opposition to the Light. There will be strong opposition to our spiritual advancement. This very opposition comes from those various souls we have alluded to earlier—souls who have consciously and willfully turned against the Creator, and promote and wreak havoc on the Earth. The need for prayer and meditation will be great, as well as the need for a stronger realization of our dependency upon our Creator. The love and light of truth will be showering down upon us, and we will, as well, be assaulted by the lies from those who would dissuade us from that truth. Discernment will be urgently required.

Now is a time when we will experience a shift of global consciousness—sometimes gradually, sometimes in a burst of revelation. It is the time of the Apocalypse, which translated from the ancient Greek, means the "uncovering," a "disclosure of knowledge," a "lifting of the veil," or revelation. We are also entering a period of *apotheosis*, which means "transforming man into God."

Most faiths have quite similar or parallel prophecies concerning our present time as a period of both great turmoil and, simultaneously, a coming Enlightenment. This is a time when humans by the millions will be remembering and realizing who we really are: sons and daughters of God, with a forthcoming legacy of eternal life. Many of our sources state that we are entering the "Age of Aquarius," which will be highlighted by an ongoing process to *lift the veil* from our consciousness, so we can fully savor and realize life—not only for now, but forever. We are beginning the process of a great change for the better.

Then I saw a new heaven and a new Earth, for the first heaven and the first Earth had passed away.[162]

Change will come about, because many new people will enter into God's Kingdom while still on Earth. What that really means is that many more people will become attuned with the Kingdom of God's Consciousness. It bears repeating that:

Know ye not that ye are the temple of God, and that the spirit of God dwelleth in you?[163]

One of the Keys to God's Kingdom is the magnificent outpouring of love—love and goodness being primary characteristics of our Creator. Once we have forgiven others and ourselves for all past errors, we can amplify the flow of love through our being by radiating it out to all people in our world. This is a key to our spiritual progress.

Annalee Skarin, in her wonderful book *Ye Are Gods*, tells us how to send out love to all in our world:

With an understanding of this great and perfect gift of love [from God] one learns the power of using his mind, his heart, and soul as one, to send it forth. Controlling one's thoughts is no longer a struggling burden of trying to eliminate the undesirable thoughts, but becomes a practice of keeping the perfect thoughts of love always there.[164]

A lot is converging in our current time frame—*all for our transition from believing to knowing—so we may experience a new, transcendental consciousness!*

AFTERWORD

While working on this book, I would occasionally ask myself if indeed, the afterlife will provide for people the experiences described herein. After much contemplation of the findings, I definitely believe that for some portion of our afterlife experience, almost everyone will experience the wonderful aspects described, which will ultimately lead to ever-higher, more profound joys. Those relatively few who don't will have led such helpful and loving Earth lives that they may instead go directly to higher realms beyond the Summerland levels described, which offer even more indescribable beauties and joys. Or, it is possible that on rare occasions there may be a soul who does not make it. If that is the case, these relatively few souls who have lived lives so totally and consistently opposed to God's Will, who refuse to ever reform, and who carry no resemblance to any goodness, forego temporary purgatory or hellish conditions, and due to overwhelming karma and God's mercy, have their energies reconstituted back to the universe.

As to the issues of the eternity of Creation and the immortality of the soul, there are innumerable reports from the afterlife that life is indeed eternal. There is overwhelming evidence that we *will* be entering a wonderful afterlife environment where there exists order, beauty, joy, purpose, peace and above all, love. Souls report that they experience a feeling of permanence, and that an atmosphere of continuity and permanence pervades throughout all of the afterlife realms. We have reports of higher souls descending to visit souls in the Summerland region confirming that this is true—that life is a constant progression without limit, that it is eternal and becomes more and more fulfilling without end. And, purely in the realm of human logic, life wouldn't make sense without an eternal purpose.

Truth, indeed, is held in the highest regard by all higher spiritual souls, and their various descriptions of how life continues and how we continually evolve are most promising. In the end, proof to any individual is really how they personally interpret the available evidence.

In addition to the abundance of information that in all likelihood (due to its consistency and logic) has been brought to us from temporary or more permanent residents of the afterlife, let us also realize and remember that our consciousness is an energy field, and that physics has established that energy cannot be created or destroyed—it can only change form. That, in and of itself, can be viewed as a tantalizing indication. Yes, our physical bodies disintegrate after "death," but not our consciousness. Numerous out-of-body experiments have proven that consciousness can exist outside of the physical form. Our physical brain *mediates* consciousness but does not actually generate it.

Words are significantly limited in their ability to describe the full experience of a soul after "death." Some afterlife sources describe being able to see 360 degrees around an object, the ability to see inside an object, and the ability to see very long distances using a form of telescopic vision. They describe telepathy, instant teleportation, revisiting the Earth, and visiting both "Hell" and Higher Realms where feelings, be they good or ill, are intensified. And, as we have been repeatedly reminded by both afterlife "visitors" as well as residents, words are inadequate in attempting to describe colors, plants, music, healing processes, and the many wonderful aspects of water. These and other experiences are things that we just cannot "know" until we experience them for ourselves. The numerous efforts to describe these things that have been sent to us by loving souls are greatly appreciated—and it is much better to have them than nothing at all!

Julia Ames expresses the limitations of words in describing the afterlife:

Now as the full-grown finds it impossible to explain the conceptions of philosophy or of science to the child in the cradle, so it is impossible for those of us who have attained to the life beyond to explain so that you can understand the fuller life which lies before the human race. Hence, when I have undertaken to tell you the truth about life here and hereafter, I do not mean that I shall tell you all the truth even as I perceive it, much less all the truth that is to be perceived hereafter.[165]

It is not surprising, but nevertheless noteworthy, that descriptions of various afterlife topics do not always agree! Apparent contradictions may all be true, as there is essentially no limit to different possibilities. In other words, the environments described in this book most certainly do not cover all possibilities. This book is an effort to record descriptions that a large body of afterlife reporters have conveyed to us, by one means or another. The descriptions can, in the least, be considered a good starting point for further research.

With God all things are possible.[166]

According to your faith be it unto you.[167]

I encourage any readers who want to learn more about these subjects to do the research. The afterlife is about our inevitable (and imminent!) future. Surely it deserves our most earnest attention.

APPENDICES

APPENDIX A

THE PURITY AND ACCURACY
OF OUR SOURCES

There are numerous categories of sources for obtaining information about the afterlife. The various categories include: out-of-body experiences; remote viewing; hypnotism; deathbed visions; after-death contacts; materializations; children, especially very young children, who remember past lives; and others.

The two categories predominantly used in this book are telepathic or automatic writing and near-death experiences (NDEs). The writing is made possible by the ability of the writer to receive telepathic impressions from external spirits. These impressions are received either consciously without deliberation by the writer, or "automatically" without conscious thought or deliberation.

An NDE is defined as a person being clinically "dead" for what is usually a short time. In an NDE the individual's vital signs cease, meaning there is no detectable heartbeat or breathing. In emergency room parlance this is a phenomenon known as "flatlining," whereby the light beam on an oscillating screen (of either an electrocardiogram which measures heart activity, or an electroencephalogram [EEG] which measures brain activity) suddenly shows no variation and, in effect, goes flat. At some point the NDE is over, and the patient, often quite suddenly, begins to exhibit physical signs of life again.

There are several NDE experiences that are considered rather typical for those who undergo this phenomenon, including the patient viewing their own "dead" physical body from an objective, external vantage point. This often involves the patient seeing and later accurately describing the activities of doctors and medical personnel, family members or close friends, ambulance drivers, passers-by, etc. Additional common NDE experiences include: traveling through a tunnel of light; seeing a "silver cord"—also described as a narrow light beam—that remains attached between the traveler and his physical form; seeing bright lights; meeting spiritual beings and viewing various aspects of life as it is lived in the hereafter.

Automatic writing yields the most detailed information about what happens to souls after life on Earth. This is because the souls transmitting the information aren't just visiting the afterlife for a brief time, but have "died" and usually been in the afterlife realm for some time. Although most books currently published about the afterlife are about NDEs, research for this book included the more detailed descriptions provided by telepathy and automatic writing.

Souls who have focused on goodness and purity on Earth achieve the highest and most accurate attunement with higher/spiritual sources of information. When someone selfishly thinks of themselves and not of others, whether through addiction or affliction, they are not able to either send or receive information with as much accuracy as those of more spiritual maturity.

To be as sure as possible about the accuracy of the information obtained, source materials were chosen from those who have lived exceptional lives of service to others. These are souls who led exemplary lives on Earth, and who conveyed their information through those still in embodiment who also led good lives.

Other indicators of accuracy are that what is being reported from one source is corroborated by the general consensus established from our other sources. Also, in most cases (unless we are looking for "newly arrived" impressions), it is better if a soul reporting from the afterlife has been there for a while, so they have a good overview and understanding of where they are.

Some challenges to obtaining accuracy and consistency in reporting about the afterlife are the fact that experiences on the lower levels such as Purgatory and "Hell" can be full of dreams, hallucinations, and misleading information by some inhabitants of those lower levels. At the same time, higher levels by their nature are "farther away" from our level, not necessarily by distance, but by vibratory level, which can sometimes make accurate communications more challenging.

Another aspect to consider is simply the unlimited variability of all the different lives that are lived—the unlimited range of experience that is possible. Due to the free will that God has given us, souls may make good or poor choices regarding their particular focus on any number of areas in life. The result is that souls have tremendously different life experiences, and have developed a wide range of belief systems, which influence their afterlife experience.

Julia Ames reported the following about the varieties of experiences reported:

The spirits...will make very different statements. They will differ indefinitely according to their different temperaments and the manner of soul they are....

They will make statements that will differ so much as to confuse those who think that the infinite multitude of individual experiences can all find a single expression. There will be any number of creeds based upon after-death experiences, which vary according to the character of the individual.

The man finds this world [the afterlife] very much what he has made of it. We all make what we live in. And as everyone makes a different future life for himself they will all give you different versions of the life they lead....

But...they will all tell you that death is a transition rather than a transformation.... There is, no doubt, a change. But it is of circumstance rather than of character. The memory appears to be quickened rather than dulled. The mind sees more clearly.

The phantasmagoria of matter disappears, and the masks and masquerading that conceal the truth dissolve away—that is important and that is universal.[168]

Let's look in more detail at the purity of some of our information sources, those I have focused upon in reporting on the afterlife.

First, we have Monsignor Robert Hugh Benson (1871–1914), the communicator in the afterlife, and Anthony Borgia, the medium/receiver on Earth who recorded Benson's messages. Benson was the son of Edward White Benson, Archbishop of Canterbury (1829–1896). During his life on Earth, Benson was a priest. He had a psychic ability, which he found to be disturbing, since it conflicted with his orthodox beliefs, because the church believed that such things were of the devil. After passing, he realized that he had missed a great opportunity to help others by using his psychic ability, and he regretted that some of his writings while on Earth conflicted with what he later realized was spiritual reality. It was due to Benson's strong sense of regret—of wanting to right his wrong—that he was given the dispensation to be able to communicate clearly to his friend Mr. Borgia. Anthony Borgia (1896–1989), the receiver, was a gifted and well-known medium.

Julia Ames, (1861–1891) a well-respected journalist and editor during her time on Earth, was the source of *Letters from Julia*, published in 1897. This book was very popular and was reprinted six times in England. Julia's afterlife reporting was received by her friend, William Stead (1849–1912), a well-known British investigative journalist and gifted medium. Mr. Stead had this to say about his ability to do automatic writing:

I vouch for my absolute belief in the authenticity of the communications received through my hand. I am positive that the letters did not proceed from my conscious mind. Of my un-conscious mind I am, of course, unconscious. But I can hardly imagine that any part of my unconscious self would deliberately practice a hoax upon my conscious self about the most serious of all subjects, and keep it up year after year with the utmost appar-ent sincerity and consistency. The simple explanation that my friend who has passed over can use my hand as her own seems much more natural and probable.

I have many friends who, being still in their bodies, can write with my hand automatically at any distance. If this capacity be inherent in the soul of man, independent of the body, when incarnate in flesh, why should it perish when the bodily vesture is laid aside like a worn-out garment?... If my friends' minds do not need to use their own hands to write to me but can control my hand for that purpose while they are still in the physical body, why should they lose that faculty merely because they have put on a spiritual body?[169]

Next, we have Sister Frances Banks (1893–1965), who was the source, the communicator in the afterlife, for *Testimony of Light,* first published in 1969. This classic has re-mained in print ever since. Even in her youth Frances was strongly focused on spiritual life. She vowed to find the truth wherever it was hidden, even if it was hidden "within the Cen-ter."

Frances was a Sister in the Anglican Community of the Resurrection who worked in South Africa for twenty-five years, first as a teacher, then as the school principal at a teacher's college. She had questions about some of the teach-ings in her Anglican church and left the sisterhood. She re-turned to England where she studied new thought literature and was the author of several books on psychology. While still on Earth she wrote *Frontiers of Revelation,* which is considered a classic. She lectured for the Churches' Fellowship for Psy-chical and Spiritual Studies. She also co-founded a group for the practice of "Group Meditation for World Goodwill." Though suffering great pain from cancer near her death, she refused all drugs. At her memorial service, she was visibly seen by several people in her nun's habit.

Helen Greaves, who recorded Frances Bank's reporting from the afterlife, states in her Biographical Introduction to Banks:

This work of telepathy and communication "between the worlds" was not a work of my choosing. The extra-sensory perceptions of clairaudience and telepathy which have been developed into a receiving-set for these communications were never sought by me. I do not use these perceptions professionally, or for personal gain of any sort.
Frances Banks was an intimate friend of mine. For the last eight years of her life we worked together psychically and spiritually.[170]

Lieut.-Col. R. M. Lester, Founder and Vice-President of The Churches' Fellowship for Psychical & Spiritual Studies (Lincolnshire, UK) had known both Helen Greaves and Frances Banks very well. He described Greaves as quite knowledgeable in being able to penetrate the "next dimension of consciousness." Lester also states that Sister Frances Banks was held in great esteem by everyone who knew her, and that it was quite understandable that she would be in contact with Greaves, since they knew each other so well on Earth.

Those of us who know both Helen Greaves and Frances Banks so well are impressed by the authenticity of these scripts. The phrasing and content of the communications are so typical of Frances, and completely unlike the style of writing as shown by the "author" [Greaves] in her previous books and articles.[171]

Lester also describes the overall message that Banks has to share, which is that "death" is but a "gentle passing" into a life that is much fuller and freer. Banks' comments on her afterlife experience in the book *Testimony of Light* are quite inspirational—a thorough reading of that entire book is highly recommended.

The Reverend G. Vale Owen (1869-1931) was the receiver of messages from several souls, many contained in his very popular work, *The Life Beyond the Veil,* originally published in 1920. He was the vicar of Orford, England during the time of his writing. Owen became famous throughout the United Kingdom through the publication of his work, which enjoyed widespread popularity. Reverend Owen was described as having a "Christ-like nature." The following appeared in an article printed in *The London Daily Mail,* June 16, 1920:

When he left the church Mr. Vale Owen was surrounded by men and women who grasped him by both hands. Men bared their heads and a number of women wept. When Mr. Vale Owen freed himself, he stood on the steps and to the hushed assemblage addressed a few simple words. As he descended the steps hundreds of people again rushed to greet him.... Thousands of people have written to Mr. Vale Owen congratulating him on his writings. Many people in yesterday's congregations traveled specially from the north of England, Manchester and Leeds in particular, to hear his address.[172]

What has happened since 1920? Why are so many of these inspiring messages from long ago no longer popular? In part this is likely because an entire century has gone by since many of these messages were published. Also, though the subject of the afterlife is still of great interest, most books on the subject are about near-death experiences. The large number and variety of NDE's, including the fact that several have been made into Hollywood films, has perhaps to some degree eclipsed the older afterlife sources.

Other possible factors are: certain well-known scientists claiming that God does not exist; a degree of "dumbing down" in the general public due to mind-fogging diets with poor nutrition and chemical additives, as well as information overload from the media. Also, we note the rise in atheism, whereby people no longer look to God, our Creator and the Source of Life, for direction, hope and love, thus blocking His entrance into their lives.

There is also the belief in some religious groups that no further revelation can be received, that once the Bible was written (or the sacred texts of other religions), that no further new information can be trusted. In this regard, we refer to a high soul by the name of Zabdiel, who provided, through Reverend Owen, several insights as to why humans resist revelations about the afterlife.

The world is suspicious of one who claims more than they can understand. They believe when they read, "I am Gabriel who stand in the Presence," because that was said long ago. But if I should say to you, "I am Zabdiel who come to you from High Places with a message from those who are accounted in the Heavenly Realms as Holy Ones and Princes of Love and Light"— well, you, know, my friend and charge, what shape their lips would take. And so I pray you let me speak, and judge me and us by what message I am charged with whether it be true and high or no—and it will suffice for you and for me. One day, dear friend, you shall look on me as I am, and know me better in that day, and be glad.[173]

It makes sense that high souls in the afterlife are very interested in delivering help to us while we dwell in the relative darkness of Earth. They continue to try to bring vital information to us because of their love for us. They know very well that souls who make their transition in ignorance of the afterlife require much more care when they first arrive than those who are informed.

Loving, selfless service is the true nature of all souls. Though it is often buried in the minds and hearts of those in embodiment by countless distractions, stress and suffering, it shines brightly in the souls who have escaped Earth's bonds and have risen to the Summerland or higher realms.

Even though it is a joy, it still takes some effort for souls in the afterlife to get their helpful messages to us. Reverend Owen's mother remarked on this:

In order to help those who still doubt us and our mission and message, let me say that we do not lightly leave our beautiful home to come down into the mists that surround the Earth sphere. We have a mission and a work in hand, which someone must do, and there is joy in the doing of it.[174]

Returning to the authenticity of Reverend Owen—Mr. H. W. Engholm, the editor of Owen's work, reported the following about the character of Reverend Owen:

To Mr. Vale Owen the authenticity of the messages is not only a vital matter but also a fact that means everything to him. He, I know, realizes only too well the tremendous responsibility that falls upon him in permitting them to be given to the world. But to know the Vicar of Orford gives one a deep insight into the spiritual side of these matters. Without seeking any gain for himself he has regarded it a bounden duty to his faith to associate his name with these messages, and to know G. V. O. as I know him, is to realize that he has done this in all humility.

It is in spiritual comradeship and with implicit faith in those who have thought fit to use him as their instrument that he has labored. No life could be more simple than the one which the Vicar and his family lead in the Vicarage at Orford, and to witness their struggle to make both ends meet on the stipend granted by the Church should be a sufficient answer to those who have been so ready to suggest that his unavoidable fame has brought affluence and ease.[175]

The following is an obviously earnest and heartfelt statement by Reverend Owen, regarding how he received his communications for his writing, and why he believed them to be true:

I do not see nor hear my communicators with bodily organs of eye and ear. The method adopted may perhaps be described as impressional. The impression, however, was so strong as to induce me to devote many hours a week, month after month, to the writing down of what came through to me in this way.

As the messages proceeded, my confidence in their authenticity gradually increased. This confidence was confirmed by communications sent to me through other people of psychic faculties of various kinds. Those quite independent lines of testimony all converged on the script and constituted so strong a case as to prove to me: 1) that the titles had been given from people who all had passed into the larger realm of spirit; 2) that these people were the individuals they claimed to be; 3) that I had taken down their messages correctly. I came to the conclusion that to reject such proof would be to discount the value of all that the world accepts as evidence of fact. Then, and then only, did I feel myself justified in undertaking the responsibility of giving this script to the public.[176]

Regarding the authenticity of NDEs, Dr. Melvin Morse has published numerous scientific articles in medical journals during his career. He has researched NDEs for over twenty years and his conclusion is that they are very real, and even quite normal and altogether natural experiences. He concludes that NDEs are definitely not caused by the brain being deprived of oxygen, or by drugs.[177]

Dr. Morse's research group at the University of Washington and Seattle Children's Hospital published this information in the American Medical Association's Pediatric journals in 1983, 1985 and 1986. Their studies have been duplicated around the world by notable institutions, including the University of Florida, Boston Children's Hospital, and the University of Ultrech in the Netherlands.

APPENDIX B

NEXT BOOK
FROM HEAVENLIGHT PRESS

As Emanuel Swedenborg and others have stated, inner spiritual feelings of joy and bliss expand and grow as we make progress on our spiritual journey, offering new experiences beyond description. This applies to those of us on Earth as well as souls in the afterlife.

With discipline comes freedom, and as we become mature "disciples" of God, we can be blessed with a greater immersion in the flow of Divine Loving Energy. To that end, we are in the process of gathering the best information available that clearly explains an accelerated path for spiritual growth. It is a great joy to do this kind of research, as it is true for all of us that "we become what we focus on." The discovery and assimilation of these concepts and the practice of these techniques is truly a blessing.

For updates on the release date
of this new publication, periodically check in at:
www.HeavenLightPress.com

If you enjoyed this book,
please post a review on Amazon,
and share it with your friends. Thank you!

APPENDIX C

AUTHOR'S PRAYER

In 2015, at the beginning stages of this project, this prayer was composed and given at regular intervals during the creation of this book.

Beloved Heavenly Father,

I call to Thee and to all in the spiritual hierarchy who would guide and assist me. Help me to find and accurately express the highest and most important information that we here on Earth need to know about the afterlife, spiritual law, and spiritual life. Reveal the best ways to prepare now for our inevitable transition to the other side—so that we may build a better life for all those in our world here, in the next world, and for ourselves.

Let me write simply and truthfully. Let this information become widely known and be a notification to those who would do evil that Divine Justice most assuredly awaits us all. And let us no longer fight each other in thy name. Grant to all who would raise themselves up the power of discernment between truth and error to help illuminate the path back Home. Let it be done according to Thy Holy Will.

Thank you,

Amen.

APPENDIX D

BIBLIOGRAPHY

Alexander, Eben, M.D. *Proof of Heaven.* New York: Simon & Schuster, 2012.

Ballard, Stan A. & Roger Green. *The Silver Birch Book of Questions and Answers.* Guildford, UK: White Crow Books, 1998.

Barker, Elsa. *Letter from a Living Dead Man.* London: William Rider & Son, 1914; and *War Letters from a Living Dead Man.* New York: Mitchell Kennerly, 1915.

Besant, Annie. *Man and His Bodies.* Wheaton, IL: Theosophical Publishing House, 1975.

Betty, Stafford. *The Afterlife Unveiled.* Hants, UK: John Hunt Publishing, 2011.

Borgia, Anthony. *The World Unseen.* Pahrump, NV: Square Circles Publishing, 2013. (Collection of three volumes originally published in London by Odhams Press: *Life in the World Unseen, More About Life in the World Unseen, Here and Hereafter,* between 1954 and 1959).

Brinkley, Dannion. *Saved by the Light.* New York: Harper-Collins, 1994; and *At Peace in the Light,* 1995.

Campbell, Joseph. *The Power of the Myth.* New York: Anchor Books, 1991.

Crookall, Robert. *The Supreme Adventure.* Cambridge, UK: James Clarke & Co., 1961.

Davis, Andrew Jackson. *Death and the Afterlife.* Boston: Colby & Rich, 1865.

Eadie, Betty J. *Embraced by the Light.* Placerville, CA: Gold Leaf Press, 1992.

Edmonds, John & Dexter. *Spiritualism.* New York: Partridge & Brittan, 1853.

Fenimore, Angie. *Beyond the Darkness.* New York: Bantam Books, 1996.

Fontana, David. *Life Beyond Death.* London: Watkins Media Limited, 2009.

Fontana, David. *Is There an Afterlife?* Hants, UK: John Hunt Publishing, 2005.

Goldberg, Dr. Bruce. *Past Lives Future Lives.* New York: Ballantine Books, 1982.

Greene, Brian. *The Fabric of the Cosmos.* New York: Knopf, 2004.

Greaves, Helen. *Testimony of Light.* New York: Tarcher/Penguin Group, 2009.

Grimes, Roberta. *The Fun of Dying.* Normal, IL: Greater Reality Publishing, 2010.

Hargis, Gladys L. *You Live Forever.* CreateSpace Independent Publishing, 2016.

Holy Bible—King James Version. London: Oxford University Press, 1611.

Hill, Napoleon. *Think & Grow Rich.* New York: Ballantine Books, 1960.

Hyslop, James H. *Life After Death*. New York: E.P. Dutton, 1918.

King, Godfre Ray. *Original Unveiled Mysteries*. Chicago: St. Germain Press, 1982.

Long, Jeffrey, M.D. with Paul Perry. *Evidence of the Afterlife*. New York: HarperCollins, 2010.

Longley, M.T. *Death*. Chicago: Progressive Thinker Publishing, 1913.

Lundberg, C. David. *Unifying Truths of the World Religions*. New Fairfield, CT: Heavenlight Press, 2010.

Marks, Jeffrey A. *The Afterlife Interviews Vol. I. and Vol. II.* Lynnwood, WA: Arago Press, 2012, 2014.

Morse, Melvin, M.D. *Closer to the Light*. New York: Ballantine Books, 1990; *Transformed by the Light*. New York: Villard/Random, 1992.

Newton, Michael, PhD. *Journey of Souls* and *Destiny of Souls*. St. Paul, MN: Llewellyn, 1995, 2000.

Olson, Bob. *Answers About the Afterlife*. Kennebunkport, ME: Building Bridges, 2014.

Owen, Rev. G. Vale. *The Life Beyond the Veil*. Pahrump, NV: Square Circles Publishing, 2013. (Collection of four volumes originally published in London by H. W. Engholm: *The Lowlands of Heaven, The Highlands of Heaven, The Ministry of Heaven, The Battalions of Heaven* in 1920–1921).

Prophet, Mark L. & Elizabeth Clare. *Corona Class Lessons*. Livingston, MT: Summit University Press, 1986.
Ritchie, George G. *Return from Tomorrow*. Grand Rapids, MI: Baker Book House, 1978.

Schwartz, Gary E., Ph.D. *The Afterlife Experiments.* New York: Simon & Schuster, 2002.

Skarin, Annalee. *Ye Are Gods.* New York: The Philosophical Library, 1952.

Spraggett, Allen. *The Case for Immortality.* New York: New American Library, 1974.

Stead, Estelle and William T. *The Blue Island and other Spiritualist Writings.* Pahrump, NV: Square Circles Publishing, 2012. (A collection of four volumes by different publishers between 1905 and 1922.)

Stead, William T. *Letters from Julia.* Chicago: Progressive Thinker Publishing, 1913.

Steiner, Rudolf. *Theosophy.* New York: Anthroposophic, 1971.

Storm, Howard. *My Descent Into Death.* New York: Doubleday, Kindle Edition, 2005.

Swedenborg, Emanuel. *Heaven and its Wonders and Hell.* Philadelphia: Lippincott, 1867.

Troward, Thomas. *The Dore Lectures on Mental Science.* London: Troward, 1909.

Tymn, Michael. *The Afterlife Revealed.* Guildford, UK: White Crow Books, 2011.

Whitton, Joel L. M.D., PhD & Joe Fisher. *Life Between Life.* New York: Warner Books, 1986.

Zammit, Victor & Wendy. *A Lawyer Presents the Evidence for the Afterlife.* Guildford, UK: White Crow Books, 2013.

ACKNOWLEDGEMENTS

Many dear hearts assisted in putting this work together. My wife, Gretchen, was a major help with editing, with ideas, and was a constant cheerleader, which really helped when facing several challenges we had to overcome. The editorial team was blessed by Timothy Connor, who made numerous improvements to the book, as well as Linda Locke, Mary Wallace, Nancy Self, Ted and Nancy Lundberg, and Stephen Peter. I appreciate the valuable feedback and ideas contributed by each of you!

Also, David Milak invested hours of time in researching several of our afterlife sources. Cynthia Frank of Cypress House was indispensable in providing helpful advice on publishing questions.

Our thanks to Tom Miller for the beautiful and colorful front cover, and to Denis Ouellette for his cover design and interior typesetting. And thanks to Bayard Lewis for his help producing a video about the book.

Last, but not least, we are grateful to God and all souls from the other side who helped inspire and guide the creation of this work. We are filled with gratitude for our blessings, including the blessing of being able to share insights and teachings from those who have gone before.

NOTES

[1] G. Vale Owen, *The Life Beyond the Veil,* (Pahrump, NV; Square Circles Publishing; 2013), 36. (A collection by Saskia Praamsma of four volumes originally published in London by H. W. Engholm: *The Lowlands of Heaven, The Highlands of Heaven, The Ministry of Heaven, The Battalions of Heaven* in 1920-1921.)

[2] Anthony Borgia, *The World Unseen,* (Pahrump, NV; Square Circles Publishing; 2013). 136. (A collection of three volumes originally published in London by Odhams Press: *Life in the World Unseen, More About Life in the World Unseen, Here and Hereafter* between 1954 and 1959.)

[3] Victor & Wendy Zammit, *A Lawyer Presents the Evidence for the Afterlife,* (Guildford, UK; White Crow Books; 2013), 1.

[4] Dr. Robert Crookall, *The Supreme Adventure,* (Cambridge, UK; James Clarke & Co.; 1961), 195.

[5] *The Holy Bible—Authorized King James Version,* (London; Oxford University Press; 1611), John 14:2.

[6] Betty J. Eadie, *Embraced by the Light,* (Placerville, CA; Gold Leaf Press, 1992), 84.

[7] Borgia, *The World Unseen,* 164.

[8] Helen Greaves, *Testimony of Light,* (New York; Tarcher/Penguin Group; 2009), 77.

[9] Borgia, *The World Unseen,* 37-38.

[10] William T. Stead, *Letters from Julia,* (Chicago; Progressive Thinker Publishing; 1913), 34-35.

[11] Owen, *Life Beyond the Veil,* 86.

[12] Stead, *Letters from Julia,* 75.

[13] Borgia, *Life in the World Unseen,* 73,165.

[14] Greaves, *Testimony of Light,* 84.

[15] Estelle Stead, *The Blue Island,* (Pahrump, NV; Square Circles Publishing, 2012), 63. (A collection of four volumes of Spiritualist Writings by different publishers between 1905 and 1922.)

[16] Borgia, *The World Unseen,* 144,145.

[17] Greaves, *Testimony of Light,* 132.

[18] Owen, *Life Beyond the Veil*, liii.

[19] Ibid., xii.

[20] Stead, *Letters from Julia*, 55.

[21] Eadie, *Embraced by the Light*, 80.

[22] Borgia, *The World Unseen*, 22-23.

[23] M. T. Longley, *Death*, (Chicago; Progressive Thinker Publishing; 1913), 24.

[24] Owen, *Life Beyond the Veil*, xii.

[25] www.goodreads.com/quotes/223330

[26] Owen, *Life Beyond the Veil*, 12.

[27] Ibid., 13.

[28] Borgia, *The World Unseen*, 15.

[29] *King James Bible*, Galatians 6:7.

[30] Borgia, *The World Unseen*, 364.

[31] Owen, *Life Beyond the Veil*, 93.

[32] Ibid., 94.

[33] Borgia, *The World Unseen*, 13.

[34] Eadie, *Embraced by the Light*, 80-81.

[35] Owen, *Life Beyond the Veil*, 235-236.

[36] Borgia, *The World Unseen*, 28-29.

[37] Ibid., 380-381.

[38] Eadie, *Embraced by the Light*, 80.

[39] Owen, *Life Beyond the Veil*, 245-246.

[40] Borgia, *The World Unseen*, 93-94.

[41] Owen, *Life Beyond the Veil*, 38.

[42] Roberta Grimes, *The Fun of Dying*, (Normal, IL; Greater Reality Publications; 2010), 89.

[43] Bob Olson, *Answers About the Afterlife*, (Kennebunkport, ME; Building Bridges Press; 2014), 88.

[44] *King James Bible*, Revelation 21:5,7.

[45] Ibid., Luke 3.6.

[46] Ibid., Romans 8:21.

[47] www.quotefancy.com/quote/891448

[48] Borgia, *The World Unseen*, 14.

[49] Owen, *Life Beyond the Veil*, 37-38.

[50] Ibid., 221.

[51] Borgia, *The World Unseen,* 361.

[52] David Fontana, *Life Beyond Death,* (London; Watkins Media Limited; 2009), 154.

[53] *King James Bible,* 1 Corinthians 13:12.

[54] Rudolf Steiner, *Theosophy,* (New York; Anthroposophic Press; 1971), 25.

[55] Crookall, *The Supreme Adventure,* xxviii-xxix.

[56] Ibid., 49.

[57] Borgia, *The World Unseen,* 148-149.

[58] Owen, *Life Beyond the Veil,* 215.

[59] Gladys L. Hargis, *You Live Forever,* (CreateSpace Independent Publishing; 2016)

[60] Eadie, *Embraced by the Light,* 74-75.

[61] Borgia, *The World Unseen,* 150-151.

[62] Stead, *Letters from Julia,* 105.

[63] Borgia, *The World Unseen,* 97-98.

[64] Greaves, *Testimony of Light,* 115.

[65] Owen, *Life Beyond the Veil,* 101.

[66] Borgia, *The World Unseen,* 35-36.

[67] Ibid., 213.

[68] Howard Storm, *My Descent into Death,* (New York; Doubleday, Kindle Edition; 2005), 30.

[69] Dannion Brinkley, *At Peace in the Light,* (New York; HarperCollins Publishers; 1995), 66.

[70] Ibid., 148.

[71] Stafford Betty, *The Afterlife Unveiled,* (Airesford, Hants, UK; John Hunt Publishing; 2011), 112-113.

[72] Borgia, *The World Unseen,* 47.

[73] Ibid., 325.

[74] *King James Bible,* Galatians 6:7-9

[75] Greaves, *Testimony of Light,* 85.

[76] Owen, *Life Beyond the Veil,* 102.

[77] Ibid., 103.

[78] Borgia, *The World Unseen,* 324-325.

[79] Betty, *The Afterlife Unveiled,* 114.

80 Ibid., 114.

81 John & Dexter Edmonds, *Spiritualism,* (New York; Partridge & Brittan; 1853), 203.

82 Zammit, *A Lawyer Presents the Evidence for the Afterlife,* 249.

83 Owen, *Life Beyond the Veil,* 419.

84 Greaves, *Testimony of Light,* 79.

85 Ibid., 98-99.

86 Ibid., 87.

87 Dr. Michael Newton, *Journey of Souls,* (St. Paul, MN; Llewellyn Publications; 1995), 87.

88 Greaves, *Testimony of Light,* 121.

89 Betty, *The Afterlife Unveiled,* 49, 57.

90 Borgia, *The World Unseen,* 27.

91 Emanuel Swedenborg, *Heaven and its Wonders and Hell,* (Philadelphia; J.B. Lippincott & Co.; 1867), 33.

92 Ibid., 36-37.

93 Borgia, *The World Unseen,* 404.

94 Owen, *Life Beyond the Veil,* 138.

95 Swedenborg, *Heaven and its Wonders and Hell,* 262, 264.

96 Olson, *Answers about the Afterlife,* 60.

97 Dr. David Fontana, *Is There an Afterlife?* (Airesford, Hants, UK; John Hunt Publishing; 2005), 462.

98 Borgia, *The World Unseen,* 162.

99 Brinkley, *Saved by the Light,* (New York; HarperCollins Publishers; 2008), 27.

100 George Ritchie, *Return from Tomorrow,* (Grand Rapids, MI; Baker Book House Co.; 1978), 72.

101 Owen, *Life Beyond the Veil,* 74.

102 Borgia, *The World Unseen,* 43.

103 Ibid., 43-44.

104 *King James Bible,* Revelation 21:18.

105 Longley, *Death,* 23-24.

106 Joel L. Whitton, M.D., Ph.D., & Joe Fisher, *Life Between Life,* (New York; Warner Books; 1986), 48.

107 Borgia, *The World Unseen,* 66.

108 Owen, *Life Beyond the Veil,* 30-31.

[109] Eadie, *Embraced by the Light,* 87.

[110] Owen, *Life Beyond the Veil,* 214-215.

[111] Borgia, *The World Unseen,* 303-304.

[112] Swedenborg, *Heaven and its Wonders and Hell,* 131-134.

[113] *King James Bible,* Matthew 20:27.

[114] Eadie, *Embraced by the Light,* 59-60.

[115] Andrew Jackson Davis, *Death and the Afterlife,* (Boston; Colby & Rich; 1865), 95.

[116] Borgia, *The World Unseen,* 339.

[117] Swedenborg, *Heaven and its Wonders and Hell,* 135-136.

[118] Ibid., 204-205.

[119] *King James Bible,* 1 John 4:1.

[120] Owen, *Life Beyond the Veil,* 625-626.

[121] Eadie, *Embraced by the Light,* 45.

[122] Greaves, *Testimony of Light,* 115.

[123] Borgia, *The World Unseen,* 386.

[124] Eadie, *Embraced by the Light,* 32-33.

[125] Greaves, *Testimony of Light,* 72.

[126] Borgia, *The World Unseen,* 148.

[127] Eadie, *Embraced by the Light,* 71.

[128] *King James Bible,* Luke 6:21.

[129] Owen, *Life Beyond the Veil,* 50.

[130] Borgia, *The World Unseen,* 144-145.

[131] Ibid., 105-106.

[132] Ibid., 115.

[133] Ibid., 116.

[134] Ibid., 14-15.

[135] Brian Greene, *The Fabric of the Cosmos,* (New York; Knopf; 2004).

[136] Owen, *Life Beyond the Veil,* 212.

[137] Swedenborg, *Heaven and its Wonders and Hell,* 265-266.

[138] Ibid., 266-267, 269.

[139] Godfre Ray King, *Original Unveiled Mysteries,* (Chicago; Saint Germain Press; 1982), 11-12.

[140] Ibid., 12.

[141] Greaves, *Testimony of Light,* 113.

[142] Stan A. Ballard & Roger Green, *The Silver Birch Book of Questions and Answers,* (Guildford, UK; White Crow Books/Spiritual Truth Press; 1998), 162.

[143] Swedenborg, *Heaven and its Wonders and Hell,* 271-272.

[144] *King James Bible,* 1 Corinthians 15:41.

[145] Stead, *Letters from Julia,* 42.

[146] Borgia, *The World Unseen,* 322.

[147] *King James Bible,* 1 Corinthians 2:9.

[148] Ibid., Matthew 7:12.

[149] Eadie, *Embraced by the Light,* xvii.

[150] Ibid., 49-50.

[151] Elsa Barker, *Letters from a Living Dead Man,* (London; William Rider & Son; 1914), 100.

[152] C. David Lundberg, *Unifying Truths of the World's Religions*, (New Fairfield, CT; Heavenlight Press, 2010), 49-50.

[153] Dannion Brinkley, *At Peace in the Light,* 37-38.

[154] Lundberg, *Unifying Truths of the World's Religions,* 51-53.

[155] Stead, *Letters from Julia,* 43.

[156] *King James Bible,* 1 John 4:12.

[157] Thomas Troward, *The Dore Lectures on Mental Science,* (London; Troward; 1909), 16.

[158] *King James Bible,* Proverbs 29:18.

[159] Napoleon Hill, *Think and Grow Rich,* (New York; Ballantine Books; 1960), 32.

[160] Joseph Campbell, *The Power of Myth,* (New York; Anchor Books; 1991), 188.

[161] *King James Bible,* Luke 17:21.

[162] Ibid., Revelation 21:1.

[163] Ibid., 1 Corinthians 3:16.

[164] Annalee Skarin, *Ye Are Gods,* (New York; The Philosophical Library, 1952), 176.

[165] Stead, *Letters from Julia,* 110.

[166] *King James Bible,* Matthew 19:26.

[167] Ibid., Matthew 9:29.

[168] Stead, *Letters from Julia,* 80-81.

[169] Ibid., 6-7.

[170] Greaves, *Testimony of Light,* xix.

[171] Ibid., xiii-xiv.

[172] *The London Daily Mail,* June 16, 1920.

[173] Owen, *The Life Beyond the Veil,* 150.

[174] Ibid., 27.

[175] Ibid., xvii.

[176] Owen, pp. 6-7

[177] Eadie, *Embraced by the Light,* xiv.

Printed in Great Britain
by Amazon

45105979R00158